Quality Mentoring *for* Novice Teachers

The **Association of Teacher Educators** was founded in 1920 as a national individual-membership organization dedicated to the improvement of teacher education for both school-based and postsecondary teacher educators. Its mission is to improve the effectiveness of teacher education through leadership in the development of quality teacher-preparation programs, by analyzing issues and practices relating to professional development, and by providing opportunities for the personal and professional growth of its members. The Association serves as a national voice for issues related to preservice, graduate, and in-service teacher education, providing opportunities for professional development through its publications, conferences, workshops, and academies.

Kappa Delta Pi, International Honor Society in Education, was founded in 1911. Dedicated to scholarship and excellence in education, the Society promotes among its intergenerational membership of educators the development and dissemination of worthy educational ideas and practices, enhances the continuous growth and leadership of its diverse membership, fosters inquiry and reflection of significant educational issues, and maintains a high degree of professional fellowship.

Key to the fulfillment of the mission is the Society's publications program. Kappa Delta Pi's journals, newsletters, books, and booklets address a wide range of issues of interest to educators at all stages of the profession.

Quality Mentoring *for* Novice Teachers

Editors
Sandra J. Odell,
University of Nevada, Las Vegas
and Leslie Huling,
Southwest Texas State University

ASSOCIATION OF TEACHER EDUCATORS
Washington, D.C.

KAPPA DELTA PI
International Honor Society in Education
Indianapolis, Indiana

2000

Direct all inquiries to the Director of Publications Development,
Kappa Delta Pi, 3707 Woodview Trace, Indianapolis, Indiana 46268-1158.

Project Editor: Grant E. Mabie

Editors: Juli Knutson
Karen L. Allen

Text and Cover Design: Angela Bruntlett
Karen L. Klutzke

Library of Congress Cataloging-in-Publication Data

Quality mentoring for novice teachers/editors, Sandra J. Odell and Leslie
Huling.
      p. cm.
   Includes bibliographical references.
   ISBN 0-912099-37-2
      1. Mentoring in education—United States. 2. First year teachers—
Training of—United States. 3. Teachers—In-service training—United
States. I. Odell, Sandra J., 1949– II. Huling-Austin, Leslie, 1953–

LB1731.4 .Q82 2000
370'.71'55—dc21
00-020424

CIP

Printed in the United States of America
   00 01 02 03 04   5 4 3 2 1

Call Kappa Delta Pi International Headquarters (800-284-3167) to order.
Quantity discounts apply for more than 20 copies.
KDP Order Code 532

Reviewers

Kappa Delta Pi and the Association of Teacher Educators wish to express their sincere appreciation to the following individuals for reviewing portions of this book in the manuscript stage:

Mary C. Clement
Berry College
Mount Berry, Georgia

Raymond J. Dagenais
Illinois Mathematics and Science Academy
Aurora, Illinois

Billie J. Enz
Arizona State University
Tempe, Arizona

Michelle R. Howard-Vital
University of North Carolina—Wilmington
Wilmington, North Carolina

Margaret F. Ishler
University of Northern Iowa
Cedar Falls, Iowa

Karen Peterson
Governors State University
Park Forest, Illinois

Patricia H. Phelps
University of Central Arkansas
Conway, Arkansas

F. Morgan Simpson
Auburn University—Montgomery
Montgomery, Alabama

Jian Wang
University of Nevada, Las Vegas
Las Vegas, Nevada

Contents

Foreword

This book is probably ahead of its time, given the tardiness of our nation's policy makers in fully realizing and accepting the need for mentoring and teacher induction that leading thinkers in the profession have advocated for a least two decades. After all, as Barry Sweeny and Gary DeBolt note in Chapter 10, only 28 states had state-mandated teacher-induction programs as recently as 1998, and even some of those programs suffered from inadequate funding. Still, in another sense, the book is absolutely timely, because the national movement toward teacher induction is proceeding irresistibly toward positive conclusion, and the need for leadership, direction, and examples has never been greater. This work provides all three.

I remember well when the need for quality mentoring practices for new teachers was made abundantly clear to me. Our North Carolina State Board of Education had called a meeting of some of the graduates for our Teaching Fellows Program. Students in that state scholarship program are selected for their intelligence, their outstanding high school records, and their determination to become master teachers. These graduates have proven to be the best and the brightest that our state has to offer, and they have collectively made a difference as they flowed into our teaching force. Their training includes year-round programs and travel designed to imbue these graduates with a sophistication beyond their years. Our state board guessed correctly, it seems to me, that, if any single individual could isolate for them the major problems new teachers endure, it would be one of those Teaching Fellows graduates in their first few years of teaching.

One after the other, the Teaching Fellows graduates testified. They painted a woeful picture of being thrown into situations in which they felt totally lost; of being assigned all of the extra duties that other teachers didn't want, including being building representative for professional associations; of running into rebellious students whom they were actually afraid to attempt to discipline; of weary administrators whose one aim seemed to be to avoid rocking the boat or drawing attention from the central office. Their elementary group cry was, "Give me someone to whom I can turn. Don't leave me alone in this profession that I barely understand."

Since that timely meeting, North Carolina has joined the ranks of those states mandating a mentoring plan. It has joined those states recognizing that new teacher graduates have but completed the first step in a career-long pursuit of mastery. It is among those states understanding that university faculty members must abandon their "ivory tower" syndrome and join in a partnership with local systems to "be there" to answer the omnivorous cries for help from new entrants into the teaching profession.

Other states have acted in ways similar to North Carolina. New Jersey has its "Teacher Induction Program," California its "Beginning Teacher Support and Assessment Program." As I mentioned, 28 states have mandated teacher-induction programs, and that number will grow. The ferment is national in its scope, and the need for new-teacher support is now obvious to even the most lukewarm supporters of K–12 education. Funding remains a problem. So does selection of quality practicing teachers willing to serve as mentors. So does the logistics of marrying schools of education and local school systems as they seek to implement teacher-induction programs.

Quality Mentoring for Novice Teachers is a survey of the best practices that have been identified by some of the best minds in teacher education. It will be extremely useful for individuals charged with setting up state and local mentoring programs, but it also offers a framework for favorably convincing policy makers to support teacher-induction programs. Support from those policy makers will be critical as these programs are established and funded. In that sense, *Quality Mentoring for Novice Teachers* is a most important work destined to take a key role as teacher education crosses yet another critical plateau.

The Association of Teacher Educators and Kappa Delta Pi are to be commended for their collaboration, for their insight, and for their prescience in authorizing and producing this important work. I commend its insights to you.

Barbara D. Day

Introduction: Leading the Teaching Profession toward Quality Mentoring

by Sandra J. Odell and Leslie Huling

In 1996, the Association of Teacher Educators (ATE) in collaboration with Kappa Delta Pi (KDP) created the National Commission on Professional Support and Development for Novice Teachers. The Commission includes individuals with rich backgrounds as authors, researchers, program developers, directors, and educators in the areas of mentoring and teacher induction. The commission was established to continue and extend the important focus on mentoring and teacher induction that both ATE and KDP have shared for the past two decades.

The purpose of the Commission is to provide leadership and direction for those working in the area of mentoring, particularly in regard to understanding what constitutes quality mentoring in preservice and induction programs. The intent is to guide individuals who are mentoring teacher candidates in preservice teacher-preparation programs in universities as well as beginning teachers in school districts. The specific objectives of the Commission are to make recommendations for:

- changing policy and practice as they relate to mentoring;
- improving the mentoring process in the initial preparation of teachers;
- enhancing the culture of schools into which novices enter; and
- preparing experienced teachers for mentoring.

RECOMMENDATIONS FOR POLICY AND PRACTICE

As will be discussed in Chapter 1 (by Odell, Huling, and Sweeny), the history of mentoring in preservice teacher education and during the induction years has been relatively short. Prior to the early 1980s, very little attention was given to providing structured induction or mentoring-support systems for novice teachers entering the profession. However, for most of the past two decades there has been a plethora of induction and mentoring programs developed at the state level as well as by individual school districts and universities (Fideler and Haselkorn 1999). Like many educational movements, these programs have often developed as a result of state mandates with little concomitant funding or as a result of a bandwagon approach to becoming involved without clear conceptions of what constitutes a quality mentoring program. As a result, great variation in quality has existed across programs and between states.

One Commission strategy has been to develop a Mentoring Framework intended to help specify indicators of quality mentoring (see Chapter 2). We hope that an understanding of what constitutes quality mentoring will, in turn, help inform policy development in the area of mentoring and guide those engaged in the professional practice of mentoring. In an effort to disseminate the work of the Commission, this volume is being distributed to the membership of ATE and is available to KDP members. Moreover, the book will be used at an ATE/NEA National Leadership Academy in 2000. In addition, Commission members have and will continue to disseminate information to policy makers through a variety of presentations and publications.

RECOMMENDATIONS FOR IMPROVING THE MENTORING PROCESS IN INITIAL TEACHER PREPARATION

In the 1980s, the idea of mentoring revolved primarily around mentor teachers who worked as support personnel in induction programs for first-year teachers. The purpose was to ease the reality shock novice teachers face as they move from university students of teaching to full-time instructional leaders in the classroom. As research and induction programs have matured over the years, it has become increasingly apparent that **mentoring** can be viewed productively as a *professional practice that occurs in the context of teaching whenever an experienced teacher supports, challenges, and guides novice teachers in their teaching practice.* The professional practice of mentoring, then, occurs in initial teacher-preparation programs as well as in support or induction programs for novice teachers. **Mentors**, for purposes of this volume, are those *experienced teachers who* *have as part of their professional assignment the mentoring of preservice or beginning teachers as they are learning to teach.* **Novices** are *preservice and beginning teachers in the profession.*

In traditional teacher-preparation programs, students are typically placed with cooperating teachers for practica and student teaching experiences. These cooperating teachers, of course, have significant influence over the growth and development of the teacher candidates (Guyton and McIntyre 1990; McIntyre, Byrd, and Foxx 1996). However, in our view, the jobs of university student teaching supervisors have too often been delegated to tangential, part-time individuals who are generally unconnected to teacher education programs. Moreover, there has been relatively little emphasis placed on preparing cooperating teachers and university supervisors as mentors. The Commission's Mentoring Framework is meant to help influence and guide the restructuring and improvement of teacher-preparation programs by providing indicators of quality mentoring practice for cooperating teachers and university personnel working with teacher candidates so that all of these personnel become effective mentors of novice teachers.

RECOMMENDATIONS FOR ENHANCING THE CULTURE OF SCHOOLS INTO WHICH NOVICES ENTER

Identifying indicators of quality mentoring practice cannot occur in isolation from defining the kind of teaching toward which mentoring practices are aimed. The Commission endorses mentoring toward reform-minded and **standards-based** teaching, that is, teaching that is "highly intellectual, problem oriented, and largely clinical," in which "teachers can justify their teaching decisions with principled arguments and data derived from analysis of their effects on learners" (Howey 1997, 4).

A host of national and local organizations have been in the process of developing professional standards for teaching and learning that represent new visions of student expectations, new pedagogical skills, and challenging subject-matter goals. Among these are the National Council for the Accreditation of Teacher Education's (NCATE) efforts to develop performance standards for preservice teachers and the Interstate New Teacher Assessment and Support Consortium's (INTASC) teaching standards for first-year teachers. Quality teaching and learning at high levels are consistent across these national efforts. In addition, a focus on making sense of information, problem solving, using a variety of forms of expression to represent learning, and recognizing the social nature of learning are common elements of standards-based efforts.

Our work is intended to identify ways in which quality-mentoring practices can enhance existing school cultures in which standards-based teaching is a focus. The Mentoring Framework encourages mentoring environments or learning communities in which students, prospective teachers, novice teachers, experienced teachers, administrators, other educational school personnel, and university faculty alike study and improve their teaching and mentoring practices.

RECOMMENDATIONS FOR PREPARING EXPERIENCED TEACHERS FOR MENTORING

The most significant and cost-effective component of mentoring programs, whether at the preservice or induction level, is the assignment of a mentor teacher to guide novices in learning to teach (Huling-Austin 1990). Researchers have identified some of the particular mentor characteristics that appear to support productive mentor/novice relationships (Odell 1990; Zimpher and Rieger 1988), have specified practices of mentors (Feiman-Nemser 1992; Hawkey 1997; Huling-Austin and Murphy 1987), and have declared what should be included in preparing mentors (Odell 1990). The Mentoring Framework developed by the Commission identifies and codifies the quality indicators for addressing the preparation and development of mentor teachers.

This book offers the profession a Mentoring Framework to guide, assess, and develop more fully mentoring as a professional practice in teacher education. We are optimistic that it will be helpful to those working in mentoring-program development and implementation at colleges and universities and in school districts. We recognize that optimal mentoring programs are achieved through school district–university collaborations. However, we believe that the concepts and recommendations contained in the following Mentoring Framework are adaptable to and will have utility in contexts in which such collaborations may not be feasible. We also believe that the Mentoring Framework will be useful to other collaborative efforts in support of novice teachers, such as those provided by independent school districts or regional service agencies. Finally, we wish to acknowledge that not all contexts are optimal for the implementation of the Mentoring Framework. Indeed, we encourage readers who face limitations or constraints in their local settings to be creative in adapting the Mentoring Framework to their particular situations.

DEFINITION OF TERMS

cooperating teachers: experienced teachers working with preservice teachers in a teacher education program; cooperating teachers can be considered mentors if they are studying and implementing mentoring strategies

induction: period including the first one to three years of teaching after receiving certification or licensure to teach

mentors: experienced teachers who have as part of their professional assignment the mentoring of preservice or beginning teachers as they are learning to teach; mentors study the pedagogy of mentoring

mentoring: professional practice that occurs in the context of teaching whenever an experienced teacher supports, challenges, and guides novice teachers in their teaching practice

novices: preservice and beginning teachers in the profession

preservice: time in which initial teacher preparation occurs in a university context

preservice teacher: teacher candidate in a preservice teacher education program working in a classroom with a mentor or cooperating teacher; includes student teachers

standards-based teaching: reform-minded teaching based on professional standards developed by professional organizations such as NCATE and INTASC and that is "highly intellectual, problem oriented, and largely clinical" so that "teachers can justify their teaching decisions with principled arguments and data derived from analysis of their effects on learners" (Howey 1997, 4)

student teacher: student in preservice teacher education program working in an experienced teacher's classroom as part of a teacher-preparation program at a university

REFERENCES

Feiman-Nemser, S. 1992. Helping novices learn to teach: Lessons from an experienced support teacher. Research Report 91-6. Lansing, Mich.: National Center for Research on Teacher Learning. ERIC ED 343 887.

Fideler, E. F., and D. Haselkorn. 1999. *Learning the ropes: Urban teacher induction programs and practices in the United States.* Boston: Recruiting New Teachers.

Guyton, E., and D. J. McIntyre. 1990. Student teaching and school experiences. In *Handbook of research on teacher education: A project of the Association of Teacher Educators,* 1st ed., ed. W. R. Houston, M. Haberman, and J. Sikula, 535–48. New York: Macmillan.

Hawkey, K. 1997. Roles, responsibilities, and relationships in mentoring: A literature review and agenda for research. *Journal of Teacher Education* 48(5): 325–35.

Howey, K. 1997. School-focused teacher education: Issues to address. *ATE Newsletter* 31(2): 4–5.

Huling-Austin, L. 1990. Teacher induction programs and internships. In *Handbook of research on teacher education: A project of the Association of Teacher Educators,* 1st ed., ed. W. R. Houston, M. Haberman, and J. Sikula, 514–34. New York: Macmillan.

Huling-Austin, L., and S. C. Murphy. 1987. Assessing the impact of teacher induction programs: Implications for program development. Paper presented at the Annual Meeting of the American Educational Research Association, Washington, D.C., 20–24 April. ERIC ED 283 779.

McIntyre, D. J., D. M. Byrd, and S. M. Foxx. 1996. Field and laboratory experiences. In *Handbook of research on teacher education: A project of the Association of Teacher Educators,* 2d ed., ed. J. Sikula, T. J. Buttery, and E. Guyton, 171–93. New York: Macmillan.

Odell, S. J. 1990. *Mentor teacher programs.* Washington, D.C.: National Education Association.

Zimpher, N., and S. Rieger. 1988. Mentoring teachers: What are the issues? *Theory into Practice* 27(3): 175–81.

Section I

The Mentoring Framework— A Broad View

1

Conceptualizing Quality Mentoring—Background Information

by Sandra J. Odell, Leslie Huling, and Barry W. Sweeny

We have seen great concern about guiding and supporting novice teachers as they enter the teaching profession throughout the last quarter of the 20th century. Beginning about 1982, educators, researchers, and policy makers began referring to the initial three years of teaching as "the induction years" and identified these years as the heretofore missing piece of the teacher-development continuum (Hall 1982).

Prior to that time, the commonly held view was that teachers were prepared to teach, predominantly at a university, and then were directly employed as teachers and asked to assume roles much like those of teachers who had been employed for some time by the school district. This view essentially assumed that a novice teacher entered the classroom with a "suitcase" full of the knowledge and skills needed to teach and then spent a career "unpacking" and perhaps "rearranging" the contents of this suitcase. The reality of the situation did not sustain this view. Novice teachers struggled much more than veteran teachers with virtually all aspects of teaching—classroom management, knowledge of the curriculum, instructional practices, dealing with parents. Worse, large numbers of beginning teachers resigned during their first couple of years in the classroom. Data on teacher retention have revealed that approximately 50 percent of teachers leave the profession after seven years (Schlechty and Vance 1983). Furthermore, school administrators often spent large amounts of time addressing novice teacher problems as they attempted to cope with unfamiliar challenges.

These realities extended the notion that teacher development occurs in stages. Previously, the concept of stages of teacher development had been examined by a variety of educational researchers (Burden 1980; Fessler 1985; Fuller 1969; Hall, George, and Rutherford 1977). They spoke of teachers developing through self, addressed task and impact concerns about teaching, or viewed teacher development as having survival, transitional, and mature stages. Experience with novice teachers extended the concept of stages/phases of teacher development by suggesting that the induction years constitute a distinctly different phase and that novice teachers need unique types of support during teacher preparation and teacher induction for the first one to three years of teaching.

A Snapshot of the Big Picture

Today, we have a much more sophisticated understanding of both teacher development in general and, specifically, the preservice and induction years. We have come to accept that helping novices learn to teach must be a shared responsibility among all stakeholders. Teacher development can be depicted as a continuum of at least four phases, as is shown in Figure 1.1 below.

Figure 1.1

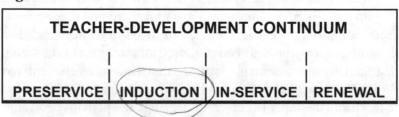

This conceptualization of a teacher-development continuum is consistent with the work of Reiman and Thies-Sprinthall (1998) and Berliner (1990), who described five levels of mastery between a novice and expert teacher:

- the Novice Stage, characterized by survival and discovery;
- the Advanced Beginner Stage, characterized by experimentation and consolidation;
- the Competent Stage, characterized by mastery and stabilization;

- the Proficient Stage, characterized by analysis and deliberation; and
- the Expert Stage, characterized by fluidity and flexibility.

Conceptually, the number and names for the stages of teacher development have varied over the years. However, the common underlying theme is that novice teachers will initially have lower level concerns related to self and the mechanics of classroom management that they must resolve before higher level concerns related to student well-being and achievement can emerge. With guidance, teachers generally progress through these developmental stages in a relatively predictable sequence. Some researchers prefer to discuss the developmental changes of teachers across time as phases rather than stages, communicating a more gradual, less discreet movement than stage theory represents. Whatever the terminology, a common understanding is that novices are unique in their needs, concerns, knowledge, and understanding of teaching from most experienced teachers. Among the interventions that facilitate the development of novice teachers as they are learning to teach, the following appear to be especially crucial (Huling 1997):

- quality preparation programs that incorporate a variety of teaching experiences in schools with mentors;
- reasonable assignments in school contexts that support and facilitate teacher growth;
- systematic induction that includes a variety of components, especially the ongoing support and challenge of a well-prepared mentor who uses effective mentoring approaches;
- clearly communicated expectations about what constitutes quality teaching; and
- teacher-assessment procedures and measures consistent with the developmental nature of learning to teach.

THE PROCESS OF INDUCTION: A BRIDGE OR A GATE?

The identification of the induction period as a distinct phase of the teacher-development continuum gave rise during the 1980s to two distinct approaches to inducting novice teachers: an assistance approach and an assessment approach. Currently, a standards-based approach has received attention as a means of challenging novice teachers in induction contexts while also supporting them. A discussion of these three approaches follows.

ASSISTANCE APPROACH TO INDUCTING NOVICE TEACHERS

The first and most common approach to inducting novice teachers focused primarily on providing novice teachers with school-orientation information, support, and guidance in the classroom, typically through a mentor. The purpose here was to ensure that the novice teacher had a successful transition into the new career of teaching and to provide professional development to assist new teachers in reaching the necessary level of skill required for effective teaching.

In assistance programs, the first few years of teaching are viewed as a developmental process, not just of entering the profession of teaching but also of learning how to succeed as a teacher. These programs sometimes exist within a larger context in which teachers are expected to be continual learners and the school is expected to be developing as a learning community. Given such contexts, induction is considered the beginning teacher's introduction to the ongoing staff-development program of the school and district. Furthermore, induction is perceived as the initial step in a career-long process of professional growth, and the induction program is often designed to establish a disposition toward that growth as the norm. Indeed, in some programs, the induction process is used explicitly to promote change in the school so that collaboration and ongoing, embedded adult learning will gradually become a school-wide norm.

The needs of the beginning teacher are addressed in the assistance approach, for example:

- reducing stress in the transition to becoming a teacher;
- learning how to apply theory and research about teaching and learning gained as a student in a teacher education program; and
- increasing the novice teacher's success and self-confidence.

In the assistance case, induction is viewed as a period that provides for a supportive transition (Odell 1990). Specifically, assistance-induction programs are designed to help the new teacher "bridge" between:

- preservice teacher preparation and the often harsh reality of the school and classroom;
- the theoretical study of teaching, learning models, and research, and the application of that knowledge in successful teaching practices that results in student learning; and

- the isolation often felt by beginning teachers from the existing veteran teaching staff.

States using this approach often give their programs names like the Entry Year Program (Ohio and Oklahoma), the Beginning Teacher Assistance Program (Alabama and Washington), or the Beginning Teacher Support Program (Oregon). As gleaned from a national survey of the states in 1998 (see Chapter 10 of this volume), there were 18 states with an exclusively assistance-oriented state mentoring program.

Assessment Approach to Inducting Novice Teachers

A second approach to induction programs involves assessment of teaching knowledge and skills. Programs using this approach have primarily focused on assessment of new teachers in order to gather evidence, through methods such as observation and sometimes portfolios, that the novice is skilled enough to be admitted fully into the profession of teaching. In the assessment approach, induction is less a developmental and more a gatekeeping function designed to block provisional teachers not measuring up from being licensed to teach the following year. On the surface, this approach may seem negative, but the gate-keeping function is necessary to the process of acceptance that makes teaching a profession. In reality, gate keeping is present in one form or another, whether through certification, licensure testing, observation, or other assessment of teacher skill and knowledge.

Induction programs using an assessment approach focus on what a teacher can do in the complex setting of a classroom and a school. These programs use the first year(s)—up to three—of teaching as an opportunity to have principals and/or experienced teachers observe the teacher candidate at work and to determine if the candidate should be awarded certification as a teacher. The need being met by this approach is that of the state and local school district to assess competency before granting individuals teaching certificates or licensure.

The names of the programs using this approach clearly describe their intent, often using "assessment," "evaluation," or "appraisal" to describe the tentative nature of the appointment period during which novice teachers are to prove themselves worthy of a standard teaching certificate. An example was the Florida Performance Measurement (FPM) System that required a team evaluation using a set of 35 state-defined competencies. The mandated use of the FPM System was halted in 1989, but some districts have continued its use voluntarily. In recent years, the number of states that have exclusively focused on a gate-keeping evaluation has dwindled.

A Standards-Based Approach for Inducting Novice Teachers

The major focus of curriculum work across educational content areas during the 1990s has been to define outcomes and standards for "what students should know and be able to do." Work on assessment of student learning during this same period has been characterized as motivated by dissatisfaction with standardized assessments, which essentially measure low-level knowledge and comprehension, and an interest in developing assessments capable of measuring higher-level thinking and student use of their knowledge in authentic applications.

In a similar way, recent work in teacher certification has attempted to define standards for what teachers should know and be able to do and to develop a set of assessments capable of measuring the ability of teachers to meet those standards. A review of state programs shows that many states have or are developing their own standards-based approach for teachers. The use of the Praxis Series of assessments by the Educational Testing Service is one standards-based assessment solution that has been adopted in a number of states—including Arkansas, Connecticut, Hawaii, Kentucky, Maryland, and Ohio—and is under consideration by additional states.

This general standards-based approach established the need to develop a set of useful teaching standards specific to novice teachers. Most notable among several creative approaches has been the work of the Council of Chief State School Officers and their Interstate New Teacher Assessment and Support Consortium (INTASC), a subgroup of some member states. As the name clearly indicates, this effort sought to create a system that would both assist and assess new teachers. In 1991, INTASC published their *Model Standards for Beginning Teacher Licensing and Development*. The response from both district and state-level programs in incorporating the INTASC standards has been swift and pervasive.

Often, induction programs combine aspects of both the assistance and assessment views. Consider that the standards-based approach for novice teaching combines the provision of new-teacher assistance with a multifaceted method for the assessment of new-teacher abilities. New-teacher self-assessment, mentor formative assessment, and administrative formative and summative assessment are all combined to provide the guidance and specific feedback novice teachers need to prompt their professional development. The dual agenda of assistance and assessment is accomplished by focusing feedback and self-assessment on a set of beginning teaching standards aligned with, and acting as precursors to, state standards for veteran teachers. New teachers are prompted to reflect on their current practices relative to teaching standards and to set professional-development goals. The mentor and the novice teacher work together to create a professional-development plan to increase teaching skills in the target area and to reduce the gap between current and desired practice. The development plan also determines the role of mentor and novice in the implementation of the plan and serves as documentation of the professional-development effort. The desired outcome is to establish a disposition in the novice teacher to career-long professional growth toward the standards.

The use of standards makes it easier to avoid the problems encountered by previous "minimum competency" approaches by setting higher standards that require career-long pursuit. In this approach, the programs are trying to address both the needs of novice teachers for support and guidance during the process of becoming a professional teacher and the needs of the state to assure the quality of the new teachers admitted to the profession. One example is the Beginning Education Support Team in Arizona that spends the first year in assistance and the second year working with teachers to help them learn how to assess and document their professional practice for standard certification.

Programs using this dual approach frequently include terms such as "Internship"—such as Indiana, Kentucky, Louisiana, Michigan, New Hampshire, New Jersey, New York, and Utah. Other states (like Oklahoma) use "Residency" as a part of their program description. A few states that use this approach identify their dual purpose directly in their program name. Examples are California's Beginning Teacher Support and Assessment Program (BTSA) and Louisiana's Teacher Assistance & Assessment Program. In all, 23 states have adopted or are considering the combined assistance-and-assessment approach for novice teachers in induction contexts with a focus on teacher standards (see Chapter 10 of this volume).

Finally, it should be noted here that we do not significantly differentiate between mentoring preservice teachers and first-year teachers. Thus, though the above discussion of standards-based approaches to mentoring has largely been set in the new-teacher context, it is directly applicable as well to the process of mentoring preservice teachers.

Where Does Mentoring Fit into the Picture?

Though numerous factors impact novice teacher development, we contend that the essence of novice-teacher development results from a combination of formal preparation and continued professional development along with teaching experiences and day-to-day interactions with mentors. We view the role of the mentor in preservice and induction programs as highly significant; the mentor's work requires specialized preparation and a significant ongoing personal and time commitment. Figure 1.2 on page 27 depicts the interaction of formal preparation and continued professional development, teaching experience, and mentoring as central to teacher development. In addition, many other experiences impact teacher development and are depicted as circles bombarding these three central influences. Though we recognize the complexity of these additional influences on teacher development, the remainder of this book will focus specifically on mentoring novices who are learning to teach.

What Constitutes Quality Mentoring?

The question of what constitutes quality mentoring for novices in preservice and induction programs has been the focus of hundreds of studies. In addition, both scholarly and practitioner-oriented products including brochures, articles, monographs, books, and videos have addressed the topic of mentoring. Almost all of these products have included various guidelines, suggestions, and recommendations about what mentoring is and should look like in practice. To date, however, there have been few comprehensive sets of standards and descriptors leading the development and assessment of preservice and induction mentoring programs and practices

Figure 1.2.

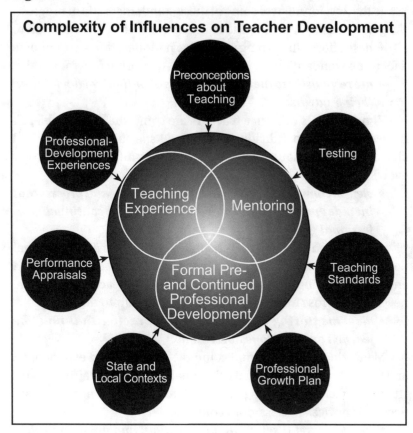

Complexity of Influences on Teacher Development

- Preconceptions about Teaching
- Professional-Development Experiences
- Testing
- Teaching Experience
- Mentoring
- Performance Appraisals
- Teaching Standards
- Formal Pre- and Continued Professional Development
- State and Local Contexts
- Professional-Growth Plan

(Dagenais 1997). This book is designed to provide such a set of standards for those working in or developing mentoring programs.

Core values for mentoring derived from research literature and collective research, experiences, study, and wisdom of the members of the Commission on Professional Support and Development for Novice Teachers have guided the current work. Specifically, we value the development of formal mentoring programs that:

- *focus on helping novices learn to teach in accordance with professional standards for teaching and learning.*

As mentioned above, a variety of national, state, and local organizations are in the process of developing professional standards for teaching and learning that represent new visions of student expectations, pedagogical skills, and challenging subject-matter goals. While the development of some of these standards is still in progress, the goal of quality teaching and learning at high levels is common to all of these efforts. In keeping with these national efforts, we endorse a focus on standards-based teaching for mentoring programs.

- *are responsive to the evolving needs of individual novices and their students.*

Though needs of novice teachers are somewhat predictable, all novice teachers are individuals who need specialized support and challenging professional-development opportunities tailored to their evolving needs.

- *view becoming a good teacher as a developmental process that includes preservice training, induction, and continued professional growth.*

As discussed earlier in this chapter, a continuum of professional development is well documented in the literature. We recognize and endorse mentoring programs that provide novice teachers the bridge necessary to cross from one stage of development to the next.

- *view mentoring as a professional practice that must be learned and developed over time.*

Mentoring involves complex interactions between experienced and novice teachers. We believe that quality mentoring also relies on studying effective mentoring practices and implementing these practices with novices in classroom contexts.

- *include careful selection, preparation, and ongoing professional development for new mentors.*

Though experienced teachers may be competent working with their students, it does not follow automatically that they will be competent mentors. Accordingly, we endorse selecting mentors using specific criteria and procedures. Moreover, opportunities to develop quality-mentoring practices must be an integral and ongoing component of mentoring programs.

- *involve experienced teachers as mentors and include mentors in program design and evaluation.*

Experienced teachers are influential role models and guides in the professional development of novice teachers. Accordingly, we endorse preparing experienced teachers to be mentors. We also endorse having teachers be site-based teacher educators who work with novice teachers and who also participate actively in designing mentoring programs and determining how programs will be implemented and evaluated.

- *are collaboratively planned, implemented, and evaluated by key stakeholders—including university faculty, school district personnel, and community members.*

We view partnerships between colleges of education and school districts as useful and powerful arrangements for mentoring programs. Partnerships have the potential to blend and capitalize on the theoretical expertise of college faculty and the practical expertise of school personnel. Community involvement is also advocated to increase the support base for mentoring programs.

- *contribute to improving school and district cultures for teaching, learning, and learning to teach.*

A mentoring program will influence the culture or context of the school in which it exists. We support mentoring programs that focus on the improvement of teaching among all participants through on-going professional-development opportunities.

SUBSEQUENT CHAPTERS

The remaining chapters of the book are intended to guide the development and assessment of quality mentoring practices. Toward that end, Chapter 2 provides readers with the comprehensive Mentoring Framework that includes indicators of quality mentoring practices across six dimensions of mentoring programs. Chapter 3 includes suggested ways to use the Mentoring Framework and provides three examples.

Section II of the book features, in depth, the six dimensions of the Mentoring Framework. Each chapter is devoted to a single dimension and offers activities to assist colleges, universities, and school systems in studying the process of mentoring. These activities include discussion questions, common problems, and vignettes with dialogue questions. An overview of state mentoring programs appears in Chapter 10, providing program developers with a summary of current induction programs across the United States.

Finally, an annotated bibliography is included in Chapter 11. Though the annotations are not intended to be inclusive of all available materials on mentoring, they represent a compilation of readings that we have found particularly useful in assisting and guiding program developers and participants in their mentoring work.

REFERENCES

Berliner, D. C. 1990. Implications of studies of expertise in pedagogy for teacher education and evaluation. In *The assessment of teaching: Selected topics,* ed. National Evaluation Systems, 21–50. Amherst, Mass.: NES.

Burden, P. R. 1980. Teachers' perceptions of the characteristics and influences of their personal and professional development. Ph.D. diss., Ohio State University.

Dagenais, R. J. 1997. Mentoring program standards. *Mentor* (Winter): 56–72.

Fessler, R. 1985. A model for teacher professional growth and development. In *Career-long education,* ed. P. J. Burke and R. G. Heideman, 181–93. Springfield, Ill.: Charles C. Thomas.

Fuller, F. F. 1969. Concerns of teachers: A developmental conceptualization. *American Educational Research Journal* 6(2): 207–26.

Hall, G. E. 1982. Induction: The missing link. *Journal of Teacher Education* 33(3): 53–55.

Hall, G. E., A. A. George, and W. L. Rutherford. 1977. Measuring stages of concern about the innovation: A manual for the use of the SoC questionnaire. Austin: University of Texas, Research and Development Center for Teacher Education. ERIC ED 147 342.

Huling, L. 1997. Novice teacher needs. A commissioned paper. Raleigh: North Carolina Department of Public Instruction.

Interstate New Teacher Assessment and Support Consortium. 1991. *Model standards for beginning teacher licensing and development.* Washington, D.C.: INTASC.

Odell, S. J. 1990. *Mentor teacher programs.* Washington, D.C.: National Education Association.

Reiman, A. J., and L. Thies-Sprinthall. 1998. *Mentoring and supervision for teacher development.* New York: Longman.

Schlechty, P. C., and V. S. Vance. 1983. Recruitment, selection, and retention: The shape of the teaching force. *Elementary School Journal* 83(4): 469–87.

2

Framework for Quality Mentoring

by Sandra J. Odell, Leslie Huling, Virginia Resta, Sharon Feiman-Nemser, Sharon A. Schwille, Carol A. Bartell, Barbara D. Day, Gary P. DeBolt, Janet Dynak, Fay A. Head, Anne L. Nagel, Alan J. Reiman, Barry W. Sweeny, and Michael P. Wolfe

To add structure and detail to the core values of the ATE/KDP Commission on Professional Support and Development for Novice Teachers, a Mentoring Framework was developed, as shown in Figure 1.1 on page 4. The Mentoring Framework is based on research and the collective experiences, study, and insight of the Commission members. The purpose of the framework is to identify and describe quality mentoring practices. We have intentionally called it a framework because it is the structure around which program developers, participants, and evaluators can add the purposes, practices, and procedures that suit their particular context. In this introductory section, we will first examine what the framework is intended to depict and then discuss several specific ways to use it.

WHAT THE MENTORING FRAMEWORK DEPICTS

A framework is a tool for analyzing complex phenomena. The Mentoring Framework is organized into six major pieces, which we call *dimensions,* as illustrated in Figure 2.1 on page 16. Each *dimension* is comprised of subparts called *components.* As the user of the framework considers any single dimension, it is important to keep in mind that the dimension does not stand alone but rather is a part of something bigger and more complex. It is the interrelationship of pieces rather than the sum of pieces that is important. Within the dimension, these components, in combination, determine the efficacy of the dimension.

Figure 2.1

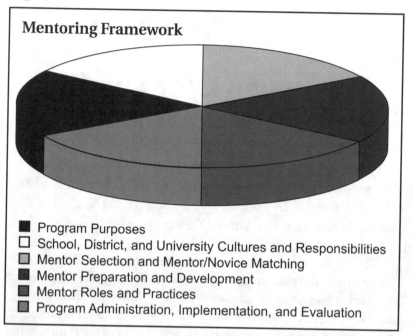

Mentoring Framework

- ■ Program Purposes
- □ School, District, and University Cultures and Responsibilities
- ☐ Mentor Selection and Mentor/Novice Matching
- ■ Mentor Preparation and Development
- ■ Mentor Roles and Practices
- ☐ Program Administration, Implementation, and Evaluation

The framework is depicted as a three-dimensional circle because dimensions are interconnected rather than linear; each dimension is important because it contributes to the completeness or wholeness of mentoring practices. Figure 2.2 below and on page 17 offers further detail on the six dimensions.

Figure 2.2

Framework for Quality Mentoring

Dimension I:	Program Purposes
Component I.1:	Underlying Purpose
Component I.2:	Refining, Adopting, and Communicating Program Purposes
Component I.3:	Utilization of Program Purposes

Dimension II: School, District, and University Cultures and Responsibilities

Component II.1: Perspectives on Teachers' Work
Component II.2: School Roles and Culture
Component II.3: University Roles and Culture

Dimension III: Mentor Selection and Mentor/Novice Matching

Component III.1: Criteria for Mentor Selection
Component III.2: Process for Selecting Mentors and Pairing Mentors/Novices
Component III.3: Criteria Used for Mentor/Novice Matching
Component III.4: Process for Mediating the Mentor/Novice Relationship

Dimension IV: Mentor Preparation and Development

Component IV.1: Initial Preparation and Ongoing Professional Development
Component IV.2: Content of Professional Development
Component IV.3: Professional-Development Activities
Component IV.4: Mentor Incentives for Professional Development

Dimension V: Mentor Roles and Practices

Component V.1: Mentor's View of Role and Relationship to Novice
Component V.2: Mentor-Teacher Participation in Preparation and Ongoing Development
Component V.3: Focus of Mentor/Novice Work

Dimension VI: Program Administration, Implementation, and Evaluation

Component VI.1: Program-Coordinator Criteria and Assignment
Component VI.2: Program-Coordinator Responsibility
Component VI.3: Program Evaluation

FRAMEWORK SPECIFICS

The remainder of this chapter maps out the particulars of the model. Substantive analysis can be found in Section III.

SPECIFICS OF THE MENTORING FRAMEWORK
Dimension I: Program Purposes
Component I.1: Underlying Purpose

- Help novices develop a professional practice aligned with professional standards for teaching and learning.
- Help novices develop a professional identity through reflection and inquiry.
- Help novices manage the day-to-day challenges of teaching.
- Contribute to a culture of collaboration and inquiry in the school.
- Provide professional-development opportunities for experienced teachers working as mentors for novices.
- Provide opportunities for instructional and school improvement.
- Prepare, select, and retain quality teachers.
- Provide personal and professional support and challenge during the initial stage of novices' careers.

Component I.2: Refining, Adopting, and Communicating Program Purposes

- Program purposes are discussed and adapted for the specific school/district/ university contexts.
- Program purposes are endorsed by school district, university, and teacher associations.
- District leaders and program participants clearly articulate and regularly cite, review, and revise program purposes.
- Administrator and mentor-teacher decisions reflect program purposes.
- Program purposes are readily available in different sources.

Component I.3: Utilization of Program Purposes

- Program purposes provide a basis for exploration and discussion of mentor and novice practices.
- Program purposes provide a basis for exploration and discussion of professional standards-based teaching and learning.

- Program purposes are regularly used to make decisions about program activities.
- Program purposes are used in program evaluation.

Dimension II: School, District, and University Cultures and Responsibilities

Component II.1: Perspectives on Teachers' Work

- The school district and the university work collaboratively to help teachers learn professional standards-based practices.
- Learning to teach is embraced as a career-long process in which professional development is ongoing.
- Mentor professional development is embraced as a necessary component in preservice and induction programs.
- Research-based knowledge is recognized as an important foundation of quality teaching.
- Teaching diverse learners to excel is recognized as an important goal of quality teaching.
- There is a pervasive understanding that learning and change take time; thus, mentors and novices must have time built into their daily work schedules for teacher development.

Component II.2: School Roles and Culture

- Focus is placed on developing a school community in which all members work to support the learning and development of others.
- Responsibility to guide novices who are learning to teach is widely accepted and embraced as an important aspect of experienced teachers' professional roles.
- Novices are given appropriate teaching assignments.
- School administrators sanction the program and regularly support it as a priority.
- Mentors help novices understand the school and community context in which they are working.
- Novices are provided opportunities to work together and with other educators and community members, both in and out of school.
- Recognition and compensation is provided for time spent in mentoring and the preparation and development of mentoring practice.

- Mentors are recognized as site-based teacher educators.

Component II.3: University Roles and Culture

- The university participates in designing, implementing, and evaluating programs.
- The university encourages and rewards faculty members who participate in the professional development of mentors and novices.
- The university encourages faculty members to collaborate with practitioners in studying the process of mentoring and induction.
- The university encourages faculty members to work with mentors to help them become school-based teacher educators.
- The university provides faculty members opportunities to work with mentors as part of their university teaching load.
- The university serves as a resource for research-based knowledge.

Dimension III: Mentor Selection and Mentor/Novice Matching

Component III.1: Criteria for Mentor Selection

Specific published criteria are used in the mentor-selection process. Criteria reflect program purposes and might include, but are not limited to:

- committed to studying and developing own practice;
- able to model standards-based teaching that the program is attempting to foster;
- able to work with adults from diverse backgrounds;
- sensitive to the viewpoints of others;
- informed about mentor responsibilities and willing to make the necessary commitment to carry out these responsibilities, including a substantial time commitment;
- committed to ethical practice;
- committed to providing both professional and emotional support and challenge; and
- have completed previously agreed-upon required number of years of teaching.

Component III.2: Process for Selecting Mentors and Pairing

Mentors/Novices
- A formal process of application and selection of mentors is followed.
- Selection and matching decisions are made collaboratively by a group comprised of experienced mentors, school administrators, the mentor-program coordinator, and university teacher educators.
- In the pairing process, mentor-selection criteria take precedence over matching criteria.

Component III.3: Criteria Used for Mentor/Novice Matching
Specific published criteria are used in determining mentor/novice matching. Criteria might include, but are not limited to:
- Teaching assignments are complementary in level and/or academic discipline.
- Opportunities are provided for novices to work with different mentors who have varied strengths in teaching.
- Mentors and novices have compatible schedules that allow for frequent interaction.
- The mentor is located close to the novice's classroom (in induction contexts).

Component III.4: Process for Mediating the Mentor/Novice Relationship
- Mentors and novices are provided with communication and conflict-resolution strategies as a component of their preparation for working together.
- A process is developed to resolve problems between the mentor and novice that they are unable to resolve alone.

Dimension IV: Mentor Preparation and Development
Component IV.1: Initial Preparation and Ongoing Professional Development
- Mentors actively participate in intensive preparation prior to beginning a mentoring assignment.
- Mentors actively participate in ongoing, formal professional development related to mentoring and learning standards-based teaching practice.

Component IV.2: Content of Professional Development

Mentor professional development focuses on, but is not limited to:

- observing and analyzing the practice of novices, with emphasis on professional standards-based teaching;
- national and local reform initiatives to enhance teaching;
- collecting classroom data;
- communicating and resolving conflict;
- understanding novice development and the needs/concerns of novices;
- fostering productive conversations about teaching and learning;
- studying the mentor's own teaching and helping the novice learn from these processes;
- analyzing the learning of diverse students and helping the novice learn from these processes;
- mentoring strategies and practices to support and challenge novices to learn at their maximal level;
- analyzing school and district contexts and their influence on mentoring, teaching, and learning to teach;
- working with novices as adult learners; and
- exploring ways to facilitate the novice's use of school, district, and community resources.

Component IV.3: Professional-Development Activities

Mentors will:

- reflect on their own experiences as novices;
- practice and problem solve simulated and/or actual mentor/novice learning situations;
- analyze and reflect on classroom teaching and learning experiences as well as mentor/novice interactions;
- receive coaching and feedback on mentoring practices;
- share and study mentoring practices with other mentors; and
- explore strategies to build and strengthen the mentor/novice relationship.

Component IV.4: Mentor Incentives for Professional Development

- The program provides mentors with time for mentor professional development during contract days of the school year; and/or

- The program provides mentors with monetary compensation for attending mentoring-related professional development conducted outside the contract day; and/or
- Credit earned through mentor professional development may be used for advancement on school district salary schedule, certificate-renewal requirements, and/or university degree work.

Dimension V: Mentor Roles and Practices

Component V.1: Mentor's View of Role and Relationship to Novice

- The mentor perceives himself or herself as a school-based teacher educator, taking responsibility for supporting, facilitating, and challenging novices into standards-based practice.
- The mentor views his or her role as a facilitator and model of self-reflection, problem-solving, and instructional improvement.
- The mentor consistently recognizes trustworthiness and professional growth as the defining dimensions of the mentor/ novice relationship.
- The mentor accepts the ongoing responsibility of building and maintaining a professional relationship with the novice.

Component V.2: Mentor-Teacher Participation in Preparation and Ongoing Development

- The mentor actively participates in and pursues opportunities for professional growth *in mentoring.*
- The mentor actively pursues individual and collaborative opportunities for professional growth *in teaching.*
- The mentor actively pursues opportunities to communicate with faculty members from universities to study research-based knowledge about learning to teach.
- Experienced mentors assist in the preparation of new mentors.

Component V.3: Focus of Mentor/Novice Work

- The mentor provides initial support and guidance to the novice before school begins and continues with frequent and regular interaction throughout the school year.

- The mentor and novice cooperatively and intentionally develop and maintain a focus for their work together rooted in standards-based teaching practice.
- The mentor supports and challenges the novice to improve his or her teaching practices.
- The mentor/novice collaborative work involves a variety of professional-development experiences—observations of one another, collaborative planning and teaching, journaling—targeted at ongoing instructional improvement.
- The mentor/novice work is dynamic; it is based on and informed by formative assessment of particular novice needs and a shared understanding of standards-based teaching practice.
- Interactions between mentor and novice are both formal and informal, occurring in and out of the mentor and/or novice's classroom.
- The mentor provides empathy and assistance to novices coping with the stresses of teaching.

Dimension VI: Program Administration, Implementation, and Evaluation

Component VI.1: Program-Coordinator Criteria and Assignment

The program coordinator:

- is committed to program purposes;
- is knowledgeable and experienced in mentoring initiatives;
- has administrative authority and expertise to coordinate university and school involvement in the mentoring program;
- has a substantial portion or all of his or her job assignment devoted to the mentor program; and
- is able to work effectively with people of diverse backgrounds.

Component VI.2: Program-Coordinator Responsibility

The program coordinator:

- arranges incentives for mentors;
- facilitates the process of selecting mentors and matching them with novices;
- coordinates professional development for mentors and novices;

- facilitates efforts between the school, teacher unions, district, and university to support mentor and novice professional development;
- coordinates program research and evaluation efforts; and
- works with program participants to schedule time for mentors to carry out mentoring responsibilities and study mentoring practices.

Component VI.3: Program Evaluation

- Evaluation addresses program purposes including the novice's learning and teaching practice, effectiveness of mentoring practices, teacher retention and certification, and effectiveness of program activities.
- Evaluation is designed collaboratively by a representative group of program participants—school district personnel, university faculty, etc.
- Data are collected continuously from a wide variety of stake-holders including mentors, novices, administrators, and others.
- Formative and summative evaluation data are collected, shared, and used throughout the year. Results are continually analyzed and provide guidance for program modification and refinement.

NOTES

3

Using the Mentoring Framework

by Virginia Resta and Leslie Huling

Just as the practice of mentoring is complex, so too is the Mentoring Framework. Mentoring is complex not only because it spans the teacher development continuum of preservice, induction, and in-service, but also because it involves multiple dimensions depicted within the framework. Furthermore, within each of the six dimensions, subparts or "components" are elaborated through a series of quality indicators.

Practitioners will find that the framework can be used effectively either holistically or one dimension at a time. In this chapter, three case examples illustrate how the Mentoring Framework can be used in a holistic way for various purposes. Example A describes how the framework was used for program design, while Example B provides a description of how mentors used the framework for self-assessment. Finally, in Example C, the framework is applied to the design of evaluation instruments for program assessment.

This chapter will conclude Section I on "The Mentoring Framework: A Broad View." Section II, entitled "The Mentoring Framework: A Closer Look," will include a chapter on each of the six dimensions. Each chapter will provide an in-depth analysis of a specific dimension and includes vignettes from both the preservice and induction levels, along with items for discussion.

THREE EXAMPLES OF HOLISTIC USE
OF THE MENTORING FRAMEWORK
Example A: Use of the Framework in Program Design

A state university recently received a grant from their state education agency to support mentoring of preservice teacher education candidates in a field-based teacher-preparation program and first-year teachers in three area school districts beginning in the fall. Dr. Rogers, a faculty member from the university's school of education, was assigned three-quarter time to facilitate the grant, and a contact person was identified in each of the three school districts and in each of the professional development schools (PDSs) in which preservice candidates were placed. Though startup time was short, Rogers decided to use the Mentoring Framework as a guide to develop the new mentoring program.

After reviewing the document, Rogers decided the immediate need was to identify mentors and to provide preparation for them prior to the opening of school. She established an advisory board comprised of the district and PDS contact persons and several of the university field-based faculty members. Each advisory board member agreed to identify the mentors from their campus/district and to involve the building administrator from each site. The decision was made that contact persons would use the specified criteria to guide the selection process.

Component III.1:
Criteria for Mentor Selection

Rogers used Dimension IV: Mentor Preparation and Development to help make decisions regarding training for mentors. She decided to hire an experienced educational consultant to provide the initial training for mentors. Because of limited training time, Rogers focused the training on mentoring strategies and skills, novice-teacher development, and needs/concerns of novice teachers. The consultant explained that the training would involve solving problems in simulated situations. Rogers set a goal of expanding the amount and scope of training in future years.

Component IV.1:
Initial Preparation and Ongoing Professional Development

Component V.3:
Focus of Mentor/ Novice Work

Component IV.3:
Professional-Development Activities

By mid-June, Rogers had used grant funds to hire a quarter-time evaluator for the project, with the understanding that a subgroup of the advisory board would serve as an evaluation task

Component VI.3:
Program Evaluation

force and help make key decisions related to the program. This would put the project on the path to achieve quality practice in program evaluation. The evaluation task force would make decisions concerning the collection and use of evaluation data.

Rogers felt that good progress had been made during the first month of the grant. She reviewed the Mentoring Framework at that point to consider next steps in her ongoing quest to move the mentoring initiative toward quality practice.

Example B:
Use of the Framework for Mentor Self-Assessment

Ms. Foster, the director of a collaborative university–school district mentoring program, decided to use the Mentoring Framework as a vehicle to analyze the program-assessment techniques and professional development for mentors. In this collaborative program, mentors were experienced teachers released full-time from teaching duties for two-year periods to mentor three first-year teachers each and assist in the university's preservice teacher-preparation program.

Foster selected Dimension IV: Mentor Preparation and Development as the place to begin, because she viewed this as an important need. Mentors spent one meeting analyzing their initial preparation, which they believed to be very strong, and identifying other types of professional development they were interested in pursuing. At their meeting the following week, they moved to a discussion of Dimension V. Prior to the meeting, each mentor was assigned to identify current practice in each component of Dimension V and compare their perceptions to identify both program strengths and areas needing improvement.

> **Component IV.1:**
> Initial Preparation and Ongoing Professional Development

In the synthesizing meeting, mentors indicated that, in fact, quality practice was occurring in mentor preparation. However, their discussions about the mentor teacher's views of role and the establishment and maintenance of the mentor teacher–novice teacher relationship led to some soul-searching and beneficial discussions. Some mentors believed that, at

> **Component V.1:**
> Mentor's View of Role and Relationship to Novice

times, their practice did not parallel the quality indicators but instead most closely resembled "a dispenser of information and advice." After more discussion, one mentor revealed that she now understood that she was functioning as "a conditional helper," depending upon the novice teacher's attitude, behavior, and/or performance. She based this insight upon the fact that her attitude was much more positive toward her novice teachers with the most positive attitudes who tended to follow her advice. Several other mentors in the room realized that, when novice teachers did not meet their expectations, they tended to respond in a less helpful fashion.

This open and frank discussion led the mentors to refocus on their role as professional educators committed to the ongoing growth of their novice teachers, even when the novices are difficult and unappreciative. This reflection led to a discussion about the establishment and maintenance of mentor teacher–novice teacher relationships.

> **Component V.1:**
> Mentor's View of Role and Relationship to Novice

The mentors recommitted to taking the initiative and responsibility for nurturing the relationship and devoting extra effort to the least responsive novice teachers.

Though the participants expected to work through the entire Dimension V during the meeting, time ran out and they agreed to continue their work the following week on Component V.3 (Focus of Mentor/Novice Work). Working through Dimension V actually took three meetings instead of one, but it led to meaningful insights about mentoring practices and how to be more effective.

Foster believed the activity was extremely successful, because mentors identified for themselves areas needing improvement that she had been unsuccessful in getting them to address earlier in the year. Her earlier efforts, she reported, were often met with defensiveness; some mentors seemed to think that this was a problem of other mentors, but not for them personally. The self-assessment process led them to consider their practice in a positive and professional manner and identify areas needing improvement. Because the mentors also viewed this experience as beneficial, they agreed to address a third dimension beginning the following week, knowing that quality mentoring programs involve the integration of all six dimensions of the Mentoring Framework.

Example C:
Use of the Framework to Support Program Assessment

Mr. Evans, the district induction-program coordinator, was told by his superintendent that the district was entering a phase of declining resources and that, in the coming year, the school board would be scrutinizing all district programs carefully before approving continued funding. The superintendent believed that the programs that would fare the best would have convincing evaluation data to support their continuation.

Evans decided to use the Mentoring Frameworks document to guide the development of program-evaluation instruments. After reviewing the document, he decided to focus his efforts around Dimension V: Mentor Roles and Practices. He determined that, if he could document that mentors were providing substantial assistance to novice teachers and that novices perceived the support as beneficial, he could salvage funding for the program. He would also use Dimension VI: Program Administration, Implementation, and Evaluation to guide his efforts.

> **Component V.3:**
> Focus of Mentor/
> Novice Work

> **Component IV.3:**
> Professional-
> Development Activities

> **Component IV.1:**
> Initial Preparation and
> Ongoing Professional
> Development

> **Component VI.3:**
> Program Evaluation

Like all evaluators, Evans faced the challenge of needing to collect substantial amounts of information and at the same time be considerate of the participants' time required to report information. He decided to address a number of evaluation topics and to collect data on an ongoing basis from various program participants.

Evans developed an activity log that would be completed weekly by each novice teacher and mentor teacher. Each sheet had seven rows, one for each day of the week. Columns were lettered and consisted of possible activities for mentors and novices, such as: (a) attending professional-development sessions, (b) lesson planning, (c) observing, (d) being observed, (e) conferencing, (f) collecting teaching resources, and (g) "other." Teachers used a check mark to indicate specific activities in which they participated during the day and, in a blank cell at the right-hand side of the page, they recorded the approximate number of minutes spent in each activity. For example, if the mentor conducted a 30-minute observation on Monday and followed it up with a 20-minute post-observation conference, he would place check marks in columns "c" and "e" on the line for Monday—and, in the right-hand blank cell, he would record, "c=30 mins; e=20 mins." If a teacher checked the "other*" box, he would specify with an asterisk at the bottom of the page what the activity entailed. By using this activity log, which took teachers less than 5 minutes per week to complete, Evans could document both the amount and types of assistance being provided by mentor teachers and could cross-check reported data by looking at the responses of mentor/ novice pairs. In addition, he could identify the amount of professional development participants received, when support was initiated, and the frequency of initial and ongoing support.

To determine how much participants valued their experiences, Evans developed a questionnaire that could be administered to novice teachers at the conclusion of the second-, fourth-, and sixth-week grading periods. The questionnaire consisted of several 5-point Likert items in which respondents indicated the degree to which the item was true for him or her. Examples of questions and their corresponding components are:

Component V.1: Mentor's Role and Relationship to Novice
- I trust that my mentor will keep my problems strictly confidential.
- If I'm having a bad day, I know that my mentor will take the time to listen and will not be judgmental.

Component V.3: Focus of Mentor/Novice Work
- My mentor regularly points out things that I am doing well and areas in which I have experienced growth.
- My mentor regularly encourages me to "stretch" my thinking about teaching and to try new approaches in teaching.
- My teaching has improved as a result of the assistance provided by my mentor.

To document the use of release time provided by the program, Evans developed a half-page form that included the date release time was used and the following open-ended items:

1. Briefly describe in what ways the release time was used.
2. Identify future activities that will result from today's work.

To facilitate data collection, Evans provided each participant with a folder containing the release time forms and the activity log for the semester (already dated), with his return address printed on the back. Respondents could complete the form, staple it, and drop it in the school mail system. He planned to supplement the data collected from program participants with other information available from district records related to teacher retention, teacher appraisals, and program costs.

Evans believed his program-evaluation efforts would serve several functions by providing useful information for both planning future programs and justifying continued funding of the program. He was also confident that his evaluation plan would not overload participants with data-collection demands.

IN SUMMARY

Recognizing that mentoring is a highly complex and interactive process, the Mentoring Framework may prove useful to educators in planning and implementing quality mentoring programs. The framework can be used holistically or to examine practice one dimension at a time. Three examples of practitioners using the framework holistically, each for a different purpose, have been provided in this chapter—program planning, mentor self-assessment, and program evaluation. In Section II, each dimension of the Mentoring Framework will be further examined and supported through vignettes and discussion items.

Notes

Section II

The Mentoring Framework— A Closer Look

Chapters 4 through 9 take a closer look at each dimension of the Mentoring Framework. These chapters are designed to assist mentoring-program developers and participants in developing, analyzing, and assessing the various aspects of their mentoring program. Each dimension of the Mentoring Framework comprises a separate chapter. Each chapter explains the dimension briefly in an abstract, followed by corresponding components and indicators of quality. Next, discussion questions are included to help users think about how the framework can guide the development of a mentoring program along each dimension to fit a particular context and situation. The discussion questions can also serve as a means of analyzing and assessing an existing program. In this case, the discussion questions should generate constructive critical examination of programs and stimulate ways to revise or change components as needed to improve quality.

A section of common problems in developing and/or implementing a mentoring program follows the discussion questions. Members of the commission who have had extensive experience helping mentoring-program developers and participants generated these common pitfalls to help others learn from their observations and experiences. The list of problems is another way to analyze and assess a developing or existing mentoring program and target possible changes.

In each chapter, two vignettes—a preservice situation and an induction-year situation—are provided to give readers concrete examples of the framework dimensions as they might be enacted. These vignettes offer views of the framework that bring each dimension to life. Readers are encouraged to think about vignettes that they might create using their own ideas about or experiences with a mentoring program. Through reading and/or writing the vignettes, readers have an opportunity to see and understand the framework through another lens. A few dialogue questions follow each vignette, which are meant to stimulate discussion about the issues the vignette raises. As a starting point for conversation about issues associated with each dimension, the questions can be used in professional-development sessions with mentoring-program participants. The key to the vignettes and dialogue questions is to use them as a springboard to address deeper issues, concerns, questions, and ideas about mentoring practices and policies in the context of the reader's specific mentoring program. Vignettes may involve more than one Mentoring Framework dimension but are included only in the chapter with the most obvious connection.

Chapters 4 through 9 are outlined as follows:

Dimension Abstract

Components with Indicators of Quality

Discussion Questions

Common Problems

Preservice Vignette with Vignette Dialogue Questions

Induction Vignette with Vignette Dialogue Questions

It is important to keep in mind that, though the dimensions are presented separately in the following chapters to look at each more closely, in practice each dimension affects the others. In a quality mentoring program, no one dimension exists without the others; they are all part of the whole mentoring experience.

4

Program Purposes (Mentoring Framework: Dimension I)

by Janet Dynak, Sharon A. Schwille, and Anne L. Nagel

DIMENSION ABSTRACT

For those who wish to develop or improve a mentoring program, few processes are as important as carefully constructing or reexamining the purposes of the program. Quality mentoring programs are complex endeavors that may include, but are not limited to, several parts: instruction for teaching particular subject matter, orientation for novices, broader induction into the profession, systematic efforts to foster instructional improvement, and other wide-ranging reform efforts that bring positive change to schools. It is essential that decisions about the purposes of each program be made at the beginning of the planning process. While making these important decisions about purposes, it may be helpful to consider the "core values" presented in Chapter 1 of this volume.

Establishing clear program purposes will help participants to develop the professional focus of quality mentoring programs. Of course, these agreed-upon purposes must be constantly refined, communicated to all stakeholders, and adopted in a consensus-building process.

COMPONENTS WITH INDICATORS OF QUALITY
Component I.1: Underlying Purpose

- Help novices develop a professional practice aligned with professional standards for teaching and learning.
- Help novices develop a professional identity through reflec-

tion and inquiry.
- Help novices manage the day-to-day challenges of teaching.
- Contribute to a culture of collaboration and inquiry in the school.
- Provide professional-development opportunities for experienced teachers working as mentors for novices.
- Provide opportunities for instructional and school improvement.
- Prepare, select, and retain quality teachers.
- Provide personal and professional support and challenge during the initial stage of novices' careers.

Component I.2: Refining, Adopting, and Communicating Program Purposes

- Program purposes are discussed and adapted for the specific school/district/ university contexts.
- Program purposes are endorsed by school district, university, and teacher associations.
- District leaders and program participants clearly articulate and regularly cite, review, and revise program purposes.
- Administrator and mentor-teacher decisions reflect program purposes.
- Program purposes are readily available in different sources.

Component I.3: Utilization of Program Purposes

- Program purposes provide a basis for exploration and discussion of mentor and novice practices.
- Program purposes provide a basis for exploration and discussion of professional standards-based teaching and learning.
- Program purposes are regularly used to make decisions about program activities.
- Program purposes are used in program evaluation.

DISCUSSION QUESTIONS

1. Develop or review the current purposes of your mentoring program. In what ways are the purposes aligned with professional, national, and state standards for teaching? In what ways do they focus on the long-term development of teachers? To what degree do they focus on managing the day-to-day challenges of

teaching? In what ways are the program purposes consistent with the research and best practices in mentoring?

2. To what degree are the various groups involved in the program aware of and able to articulate program purposes? Are some groups in need of clarification about program purposes? What activities must occur to ensure that all participants have a clear understanding of program purposes?

3. In what ways and in what contexts are program purposes communicated? How often does such communication occur? What actions could be taken to highlight program purposes regularly?

4. To what degree do initial and ongoing professional-development activities align with and support program purposes? Which purposes need additional attention through professional development, and how can these needs be addressed?

5. What measures are in place to assess progress toward the achievement of program purposes? What additional measures must be developed, and what is the plan for developing and implementing these measures?

COMMON PROBLEMS

- No written program purpose exists even though some people have a general understanding of program purposes.
- Program purposes, while explicitly stated in writing, are not regularly cited or reflected in administrative decisions and cannot be articulated by participants.
- Program administrators are the only ones who understand the program goals, because the goals are not being shared continuously with all participants.
- Program purposes focus on day-to-day challenges rather than on school improvement and the promotion of lifelong learning.
- Program purposes are not aligned with other school or district improvement efforts and may, in fact, be in conflict with other efforts.
- Program purposes may be articulated by those directly involved in the program but not by other stakeholders in the school/ university cultures whose understanding is critical for program success.

Vignettes

Preserve Vignette
Mentoring Framework Dimension I: Program Purposes at the Preservice Level

Vignette Characters: Representative faculty and administrators from a university teacher education program and a large school district.

Summary: The rationale and purpose of a mentoring program is to promote a disposition toward lifelong learning for all participants. The program should serve as a vehicle to facilitate instructional and school improvement and the establishment of collaborative norms. A representative group of stakeholders should develop program purposes collaboratively and make them readily available to interested parties.

Background and Context: Representative faculty and administrators from a university and a large school district formed a collaboration team to institutionalize a formal partnership. The purpose of this partnership was to improve preservice teacher education within the context of schools and to offer better professional development for experienced teachers who serve as mentors to preservice teachers. This vignette summarizes the collaborative efforts of the team as they worked through obstacles to conceptualize and develop a mentoring program and rationale.

Narrative: Summary of several monthly meetings that established an underlying purpose for a more formal mentoring program.

Numbering approximately 20, team participants included an equal number of administrators and faculty members from the university and school district. The commitment and active participation of the dean of the college of education, the superintendent of the school district, and representatives from both the teachers' and administrators' unions gave status to the team's efforts. One of the first tasks of the team was to develop a process for raising questions, debating practices, and seeking solutions to educational problems experienced by mentors and preservice teachers who work together in the schools. The team established ground rules including:

- Leave titles at the door.
- Don't sell your own political or professional agenda.
- Use breakout sessions to foster problem solving in small, informal groups, then return to the whole group for consensus decision making.

The team then spent several sessions establishing a common focus for a mentoring program. The group quickly agreed that, for years, they had shared the responsibility of student teaching, but without real collaboration. Each year, more than 100 student teachers were placed in classrooms around the district. University faculty members and classroom teachers communicated infrequently, and the perceived difference in importance attached to theory and practice by the two groups was evident. Accordingly, purposes for the new program were established: develop school district and university collaboration; create partnership school sites in which clusters of student teachers would be placed; and establish new roles for mentor teachers as school-based teacher educators. A new delivery system, including different roles for university faculty members and classroom teachers, was then developed to meet the needs of student teachers and K–12 students more effectively. The new student teacher system provided more realistic and practice-based experiences for student teachers, who were clustered in groups in single school buildings or in two or three buildings close together. This arrangement allowed student teachers and mentors more time to interact with one another and with the college of education faculty as they planned effective ways to guide the mentoring process.

Because the new program made the mentor teacher more directly responsible for guiding a student teacher's practice, the new program structure had to allow mentor teachers to meet on a regular basis with university faculty members. One mentor at each site would be designated as a mentor coach to provide site-specific support to other mentor teachers and work as a liaison between the university and the school. This mentor coach would meet with other mentor coaches and university faculty members each month for one half day of release time. In addition, the university faculty member who was assigned to a given cluster would meet with all of the mentors at that site on a weekly basis. Each cluster would decide whether to meet after school or during a part of the school day when the student teachers were teaching in the classroom. All of the student teachers assigned to that cluster would also meet with the university faculty member weekly after school.

The team then introduced this program rationale and plan to other faculty members and administration at their respective institutions and asked for suggestions. Based on the faculty and administration feedback, modifications in the program rationale and plan would be added to the agenda for the next team meeting.

Vignette Dialogue Questions

1. What are the purposes of the program described in this vignette?
2. What are the pros and cons of clustering student teachers in a given school on a regular basis?
3. In what ways could more time for mentors, student teachers, and university faculty to interact be built into this program?
4. How might the situation described in this vignette have been different if the school district and/or teacher education program were much smaller?
5. What difficulties can be anticipated as mentors make the transition from their previous role into their new one with additional responsibilities?

Induction Vignette
Mentoring Framework Dimension I:
Program Purposes at the Induction Level

Vignette Characters: Group of school district personnel and university representatives.

Summary: A mentoring program has an underlying rationale and purposes collaboratively developed by a representative group of stakeholders. The program purposes build upon prior knowledge and best practices of teachers, reflect district and school goals and priorities, and are clearly articulated by program participants.

Background and Context: The coordinator of staff development invited the planning group for a new induction program to a day-long retreat. Included in the group were three principals from schools that had a large number of first- and second-year teachers, three teachers with experience in mentoring beginning teachers, and two university faculty members who worked with student teachers and first-year teachers.

Narrative: Initial meeting to conceptualize a more formal mentoring program.

Recognizing an impending need for more formalized support for beginning teachers, the group agreed to design a program that would provide support for all first- and second-year teachers in the district. Group members believed that this program could be a powerful long-term investment in the quality of educational programs operated by the district. Participants from the local university were invited to help build connections between the preservice teacher-preparation program and the professional development of new teachers.

The group agreed that the major purposes for their program would be to:

- provide a systematic program of support for all first- and second-year teachers in the district;
- link the support to state-adopted standards for all teachers;
- promote a commitment to continued professional development during preservice training and throughout a teaching career;
- increase the quality of the instructional programs in all schools throughout the district; and
- promote the development of collegial support networks to increase job satisfaction and retention in the profession.

Using the recently developed state standards for teachers, the group brainstormed types of support that could help beginning teachers meet those standards. Then, the most effective ways to deliver this support were explored. Four different formats were envisioned:

1. group workshops;
2. observations in mentors' classrooms;
3. mentor observations and coaching in beginning teachers' classrooms; and
4. time for independent or small-group study in areas of identified need or interest.

The group determined that the program would be introduced to new teachers at the orientation sessions held the week before the start of the new school year. Each new teacher would receive a packet of useful information about district resources, policies, and procedures, as well as a special brochure outlining the purposes of the new-teacher support program. Mentors would be assigned, and each would be available to spend time helping a new teacher prepare for the start of school. Special emphasis would be placed on ensuring that each new teacher felt welcomed, had someone to turn to for help, and was aware of the types of support available to them throughout the year.

The district's director of evaluation services was invited to attend the group's next meeting to help design a formative assessment procedure for determining the program's effectiveness during its first year. Data collected during the first year on each of the program's purposes could help determine modifications for the second year of operation.

Vignette Dialogue Questions

1. How could your state and national standards for teachers be incorporated into purposes established for a new-teacher mentoring program?
2. What incentives might be necessary for teachers to apply to be a mentor in this type of program?
3. What would your own case vignette be like, and what details would you need to share with others in the group?
4. What preparation should mentors receive to provide effective assistance to novice teachers prior to the opening of school?
5. What could facilitate the development of collegial support networks in this program?
6. What system supports are necessary to accomplish the purposes identified for this mentoring program?

5

School, District, and University Cultures and Responsibilities (Mentoring Framework: Dimension II)

by Michael P. Wolfe, Carol A. Bartell, and Gary P. DeBolt

DIMENSION ABSTRACT

Schools are complex places—and mentoring programs are difficult to develop and sustain, particularly when they involve collaboration between schools and universities. Quality mentoring programs recognize the multidimensional environments within which they exist. Program planners and participants should examine carefully the cultures and responsibilities of both the public schools and the colleges or universities with whom they collaborate to support novice teachers. The individual school, the school district, the college or university, and the broader community in which the school exists must each be considered from the perspective of each stakeholder. Discussion of the roles and responsibilities of each group can lead to more effective collaboration and a more productive preservice or induction experience for novice teachers.

COMPONENTS WITH INDICATORS OF QUALITY
Component II.1: Perspectives on Teachers' Work

- The school district and the university work collaboratively to help teachers learn professional standards-based practices.
- Learning to teach is embraced as a career-long process in which

professional development is ongoing.

- Mentor professional development is embraced as a necessary component in preservice and induction programs.
- Research-based knowledge is recognized as an important foundation of quality teaching.
- Teaching diverse learners to excel is recognized as an important goal of quality teaching.
- There is a pervasive understanding that learning and change take time; thus, mentors and novices must have time built into their daily work schedules for teacher development.

Component II.2: School Roles and Culture

- Focus is placed on developing a school community in which all members work to support the learning and development of others.
- Responsibility to guide novices who are learning to teach is widely accepted and embraced as an important aspect of experienced teachers' professional roles.
- Novices are given appropriate teaching assignments.
- School administrators sanction the program and regularly support it as a priority.
- Mentors help novices understand the school and community context in which they are working.
- Novices are provided opportunities to work together and with other educators and community members, both in and out of school.
- Recognition and compensation is provided for time spent in mentoring and the preparation and development of mentoring practice.
- Mentors are recognized as site-based teacher educators.

Component II.3: University Roles and Culture

- The university participates in designing, implementing, and evaluating programs.
- The university encourages and rewards faculty members who participate in the professional development of mentors and novices.
- The university encourages faculty members to collaborate with practitioners in studying the process of mentoring and induc-

tion.

- The university encourages faculty members to work with mentors to help them become school-based teacher educators.
- The university provides faculty members opportunities to work with mentors as part of their university teaching load.
- The university serves as a resource for research-based knowledge.

DISCUSSION QUESTIONS

1. What evidence is there that mentors value their role as teacher educators working with novice teachers? In what ways do they view it as an imposition? What can be done to facilitate mentors' views of the professional importance of their role?

2. How is the university functioning in partnership with program participants, and to what degree are participants viewed as outsiders? What can be done to facilitate and/or maintain the efficacy of this partnership?

3. To what degree are the school's personnel knowledgeable about and committed to standards-based teaching practices? What evidence is there that mentors recognize that they must also improve their own teaching practices? What can be done to promote educators' understanding of and commitment to standards-based teaching?

4. How is time during the school day made available for mentors and novice teachers to work together? What actions can be taken to increase the amount of time they have to work together as a part of their day-to-day practice?

5. To what degree is there a commitment to ongoing learning about teaching among all educators? To what degree do school personnel value the need to improve their own performance? What benefits are to be gained from all teachers being engaged in the ongoing study of teaching? How can this process best be supported?

6. What activities are in place to help acculturate novice teachers into the community? What can be done to help novice teachers learn more about the community and feel more a part of it?

7. How do university policies, structures, and reward systems encourage the active involvement of faculty members in mentoring programs? What can be done to facilitate and reward faculty involvement?

COMMON PROBLEMS

- School and university work together on given projects, but each operates as an independent entity, failing to appreciate the realities of one another's perspectives.
- Program participants believe that only novices are in need of professional growth and fail to embrace the notion that professional growth of mentors is an important component of the program.
- The school culture is unsupportive of providing time during the work day for mentors and novices to work together or to participate in professional development, promoting instead a view that no teacher should be out of the classroom for any reason.
- The university does not reward the extensive off-campus commitment involved in school-based collaborative programs.
- Diversity is not actively promoted in visible ways nor clearly reflected in program practices or attitudes.
- Novices are provided inadequate assistance related to community acculturation as a part of the ongoing support program.
- A peer-support component for both novices and mentors is not addressed.

VIGNETTES

Preservice Vignette
Mentoring Framework Dimension II: School, District, and University Cultures and Responsibilities at the Preservice Level

Vignette Characters: Sarah, a preservice intern, her cooperating teacher at Elmstreet Elementary, and her university supervisor.

Summary: School and district culture is a powerful influence on teacher and student behavior. Culture is developed over time and affects instructional decisions and student-management practices. A preservice teacher may not be fully aware of the effects of school culture and likely will need support from both the university faculty member and cooperating teacher as he or she learns to navigate the culture of a specific school and district.

Background and Context: Elmstreet Elementary School prides itself on its quiet and orderly students. When kids walk in the halls, the lines are straight and quiet. In the cafeteria, children converse in low tones, producing only a soft hum. All teachers are expected to maintain an orderly classroom atmosphere, which permeates the building. Sarah's classroom-management preparation is participatory, child-centered, and democratic. Sarah is trying to practice her approach in the classroom.

Narrative: Four weeks into the semester.

Sarah is now four weeks into her internship and has experienced difficulty with three fifth-grade boys. The boys interrupt instruction by shouting out answers they know will elicit laughter, talking loudly while Sarah is talking, throwing things at and to each other, and making fun of other children.

The cooperating teacher used a classroom-management system that depended on the sheer force of her dominating personality. All she had to say was "Matthew!" and all three boys paid instant attention. Sarah, however, unsure of her personal authority, encountered problems with these three boys.

Sarah tried some of the strategies she learned in her classroom-management course. First, she used proximity control, which quieted them for one minute. She thought it worked but, as she turned her back, a spit wad hit her in the back. At the second offense, she wrote names on the chalkboard, indicating that a check mark by a name would mean after school detention, whereupon one of the boys declared, "I ride the bus and can't stay after school." After school, when the university supervisor arrived, Sarah burst into tears because she felt unable to manage the students.

The university supervisor asked the cooperating teacher to join the meeting and proceeded to recreate the classroom situation. Before describing the situation, the university supervisor questioned the cooperating teacher about school and classroom expectations and routines for discipline and management.

Questions were asked about the boys' backgrounds, the level of parental involvement, and any history of classroom disturbances attributed to the three boys. During the three-way conference, the university supervisor pulled Sarah into the conversation so that she too felt a part of the fact-finding mission. Once all of the information was shared, the university supervisor called on the cooperating teacher to share her wisdom and discuss successful methods she would suggest Sarah try to create a positive classroom environment for learning.

Finally, Sarah stated that using management techniques without realizing the classroom and school climate, and its expectations for behavior, was not wise. She also shared that the boys may have been testing her freshness as a teacher to determine Sarah's tolerance for behavior.

As a final process, the intern, the cooperating teacher, and the university supervisor completed a growth plan for and with Sarah. The plan included:

- Split up the three boys.
- Do a behavior contract with each boy, and establish classroom expectations for the class with the cooperating teacher's input.
- Work individually with the boys whenever the cooperating teacher is teaching.
- Keep a daily log to monitor behavior patterns of the classroom.
- Use a tape recorder to practice using a more commanding teacher voice.
- Observe other master teachers' classroom-management practices.
- Meet daily with the cooperating teacher for a coaching session.
- Meet weekly with the university supervisor for sharing and feedback.

Vignette Dialogue Questions

1. Considering Sarah's situation, what problems arise when there is a difference between a school's culture and a student teacher's teaching approaches? What position should a mentor teacher take in helping a novice teacher succeed in such a situation?
2. What is the value of helping Sarah self-identify her classroom problems and allowing her to participate in developing her growth plan?
3. What are the pros and cons of using a formal growth plan with a novice teacher?
4. What strategies would you use with Sarah to boost her self-confidence and to assure her that the mentor and university supervisor have confidence in her ability to become an effective teacher?

Induction Vignette
Mentoring Framework Dimension II: School, District, and University Cultures and Responsibilities at the Induction Level

Vignette Characters: Rosa, a novice teacher, Mary, her mentor, and an administrator.

Summary: Working conditions for teachers can contribute to or detract from their ability to provide good instructional experiences for their students. New teachers must be socialized into their schools and organizations in positive ways, keeping their novice status in mind. Structured opportunities should be provided to allow teachers to work together in collegial ways with others who share their responsibilities. A good induction program builds on and extends thorough preservice preparation.

Background and Context: Rosa selected from among three job offers to teach a third-grade class in a southern California school district. She accepted this particular position because she knew that the school district was participating in the new state-funded teacher-induction program. Though she felt she was well-prepared at the university she attended, she was nervous about beginning a year all on her own in a very challenging work environment. She knew that the program included additional mentoring by experienced teachers, workshops especially for groups of new teachers, and both formal and informal feedback about progress. Her progress would be documented in a teaching portfolio that would form the basis of her discussions with her mentor and other support providers.

Because California had reduced class size to 20 in the early grades, Rosa knew that she would have a manageable class size. When she met with her principal before school started, she was told that it was a district policy to avoid assigning combination classes to new teachers. So Rosa was confident that she would have no more than 20 third-grade students.

Narrative: First week of school.
Rosa arrived at her school a week ahead of the other teachers to meet with the principal and the experienced teacher who was as-

signed as her mentor. Both accompanied her to her classroom, which was located in a portable facility away from the main school building. Rosa was told that all three sections of the third grade were clustered together in the portables, including her mentor's class. She felt relieved knowing that help was nearby.

She noticed that the room already had some materials and equipment. Not only did the classroom have the needed desks and chairs, but Mary, her mentor, also had equipped the classroom with supplies, textbooks, equipment, and materials for Rosa to review and from which she could make choices. They went to the resource room together to select additional materials. For the next two days, Mary helped Rosa finish setting up the classroom, plan lessons for the first week of school based on the third-grade standards the district had adopted, and become acquainted with school procedures.

Later in the week, the principal stopped by to see if Rosa needed anything else to get off to a good start. The principal also explained that she would drop in to visit the class informally several times before formal evaluating took place. "Please let me know if there is anything special you would like me to observe or give you feedback about," she noted.

At the end of the week, Rosa met other new teachers in the district at the special orientation session for new teachers. The day was spent going through a "getting started" handbook prepared for the new teachers. It answered a long list of questions new teachers in previous years had asked about working in the district, provided activities that could be used at the beginning of the school year to assess students' reading and math skills, gave examples of bulletin boards that could be used in the room, and contained other useful information and ideas. At this meeting, Rosa met other new third-grade teachers from the district and learned that they would meet together once a month to share problems and ideas. She learned that her mentor would work with her in her classroom once a week.

She was given a notebook to use for the portfolio and some initial guidance about collecting artifacts or representations of her teaching. Because she had constructed a portfolio as a part of her professional-preparation experience at her university, she felt comfortable updating it during the next year.

The orientation concluded with a presentation by a panel of second-year teachers who had been through the same orientation the previous year. They talked about the challenges and issues they had faced, as well as the help they had received. They shared their first-year portfolios, talked about what they had learned in putting their work together, and reflected on their progress and that of their students. All panel members gave out their home telephone numbers and e-mail addresses, offering, "Contact me anytime." Rosa returned to her school feeling confident about the beginning of the year.

Vignette Dialogue Questions

1. What are your feelings about the initial kinds of support Mary and others gave Rosa before they met? What obstacles could prevent offering such support, and how would you address them?
2. In what other ways might Rosa's colleagues help her prepare for the beginning of school?
3. What might be the contents of the professional portfolio that Rosa was asked to construct?
4. In addition to the orientation session, what ongoing activities could be conducted with novice teachers during the first two months of school?
5. Specifically, what types of support could the mentor provide to assist Rosa in compiling her portfolio?
6. What can the mentor do to help Rosa become more familiar with her students' cultures, learning styles, interests, and needs?

NOTES

6

Mentor Selection and Mentor/Novice Matching (Mentoring Framework: Dimension III)

by Sharon A. Schwille, Anne L. Nagel, and Gary P. DeBolt

DIMENSION ABSTRACT

Identifying the process for selecting possible mentors is essential for any mentoring program. Once candidates are known, quality programs use previously established criteria for selecting mentors. It is helpful to disseminate these criteria to all program participants so that selection decisions may be reached collaboratively by representatives of the faculty, administration, and university teacher educators.

Dimension III emphasizes the benefits of using collaboratively developed criteria for matching mentors and novice teachers. Programs seldom are able to make ideal matches in all cases, but clear criteria can lend stability and reason to the process. Despite the best plans for mentor/novice matches, conflicts sometimes arise. Successful programs have plans in place to deal with conflict or ineffective matches, which enables participants to focus on the program's purposes.

COMPONENTS WITH INDICATORS OF QUALITY
Component III.1: Criteria for Mentor Selection

Specific published criteria are used in the mentor-selection process. Criteria reflect program purposes and might include, but are not limited to:

- committed to studying and developing own practice;
- able to model standards-based teaching that the program is attempting to foster;
- able to work with adults from diverse backgrounds;
- sensitive to the viewpoints of others;
- informed about mentor responsibilities and willing to make the necessary commitment to carry out these responsibilities, including a substantial time commitment;
- committed to ethical practice;
- committed to providing both professional and emotional support and challenge; and
- have completed previously agreed-upon required number of years of teaching.

Component III.2: Process for Selecting Mentors and Pairing Mentors/Novices

- A formal process of application and selection of mentors is followed.
- Selection and matching decisions are made collaboratively by a group comprised of experienced mentors, school administrators, the mentor-program coordinator, and university teacher educators.
- In the pairing process, mentor-selection criteria take precedence over matching criteria.

Component III.3: Criteria Used for Mentor/Novice Matching

Specific published criteria are used in determining mentor/novice matching. Criteria might include, but are not limited to:

- Teaching assignments are complementary in level and/or academic discipline.
- Opportunities are provided for novices to work with different mentors who have varied strengths in teaching.
- Mentors and novices have compatible schedules that allow for frequent interaction.
- The mentor is located close to the novice's classroom (in induction contexts).

Component III.4: Process for Mediating the

Mentor/Novice Relationship

- Mentors and novices are provided with communication and conflict-resolution strategies as a component of their preparation for working together.
- A process is developed to resolve problems between the mentor and novice that they are unable to resolve alone.

DISCUSSION QUESTIONS

1. What systematic process is in place for selecting and matching mentors and novice teachers? To what degree is this process widely understood by all parties involved? What opportunities do novice teachers have to work with various mentors of different teaching strengths? What refinements are needed in the selection and matching processes or in communicating the processes to participants?

2. To what degree is the mentor-selection process driven by the conscientious application of established criteria, convenience, competing school demands, favoritism, etc.? What steps can increase the effectiveness and integrity of this process? How can teachers not selected as mentors contribute to the mentoring program?

3. To what degree are selection and matching decisions made by a collaborative group or by one or two individuals? How can this process be modified to include broader representation of program participants?

4. In what ways are mentor teachers made aware of mentoring responsibilities before they make a commitment to participate in the program? What can be done to ensure that mentors are aware of the demands and willing to commit the time and effort required before they are expected to mentor novice teachers?

5. What processes are in place for resolving conflicts between a mentor and a novice teacher? Is the norm in the program to deal with conflicts openly or to fail to acknowledge them and work for resolution? What can be done to promote more healthy conflict resolution within the program?

COMMON PROBLEMS

- Mentors are asked to volunteer before they fully understand the scope and nature of the mentoring role.

- Mentors volunteer but do not submit formal applications.
- Criteria for mentor selection are specified but not truly used in the mentor-selection process.
- Mentors confuse their roles when working with novices versus student teachers. Working with student teachers may require assistance and formal assessment, while working with novices may require assistance with informal assessment.
- Matching decisions are made by a single individual rather than through a collaborative process involving a number of program representatives.
- There is no established process for addressing or mediating mentor/novice conflicts.
- Mentor/novice matching decisions are made based on convenience or proximity rather than on selection criteria related to program purposes.

VIGNETTES

Preservice Vignette
Mentoring Framework Dimension III: Mentor Selection and Mentor/Novice Matching at the Preservice Level

Vignette Characters: Latoya, a teacher applying for selection as a mentor, her principal, a field instructor, and prospective student teachers.

Summary: Mentor teachers for a preservice teacher education program are selected in several ways. Often, teachers self-select by signing up when the teacher education program contacts schools to recruit mentor teachers. Sometimes, principals tap teachers whom they think will be good mentors and will develop professionally from involvement in the program. At other times, university field instructors identify teachers from a school where they have observed or had teachers recommend a colleague. In any case, selection of a mentor teacher must be based on criteria that include a good fit between the teacher's and university's beliefs about good teaching, the teacher's goals, and the program's purposes; the teacher's ability to mentor a preservice novice learning to teach; and the teacher's commitment to developing his or her teaching and mentoring practices.

Matching a mentor with a student teacher must be based on compatibility between their individual beliefs about good teaching, expectations for students, and approach toward classroom organization and management. Though personality traits play a part in a good match, they should not be the overriding factor. With open communication, a good relationship can be built on shared professional goals and visions of good teaching without the expectation that a personal friendship must result as well.

Background and Context: The university placement coordinator and the school principal communicate frequently during the placement process to identify teachers who would be good mentor candidates. Then they must match each with a prospective student teacher who seems likely to gain educationally from being in a particular teacher's classroom. A description of selecting a mentor teacher and matching the mentor with a student teacher follows.

Narrative: Mentor selection and matching with a student teacher.

Having seen other teachers in her building working with student teachers, Latoya decided to participate in the teacher-preparation program as a mentor. She thought the extra attention for her students would be beneficial, noting that the challenges of helping someone learn to teach also would enrich her own thinking. She talked with her principal about what was involved. The principal explained that the criteria are set by the university and agreed upon by the district. She told Latoya that, though years of experience do not necessarily predict that someone will be a good mentor, Latoya must have achieved tenure or its equivalent to participate. More importantly, there are mentoring dispositions and beliefs about good teaching that characterize a good mentor. Latoya must have a vision of good teaching that is congruent with the practice that the university teacher-preparation program advocates. In Latoya's case, this meant teaching toward reform-minded practice supported by national standards identified by subject-matter associations and by the Interstate New Teacher Assessment and Support Consortium. The principal gave Latoya some materials about the teacher-preparation program and a booklet on expectations and responsibilities of mentor teachers and told her to contact the university field instructor assigned to their school.

When Latoya met with the field instructor, she had questions already in mind. She mentioned that the materials she read stressed that mentoring required a big time commitment, and she wondered how she would manage. She and the field instructor talked about how other mentors make use of time both in and out of the classroom to help their student teachers learn to teach. They discussed Latoya's reasons for wanting to be a mentor and noted that these complemented the teacher education program's goals. They discussed expectations such as participation in mentor-teacher institutes and program meetings that support teachers' development of their mentoring practice. Latoya not only got answers to her questions but also understood that becoming a mentor was a long-term commitment to working with the program to develop her mentoring practice.

Following the meeting, both Latoya and the field instructor told the principal that they were interested in Latoya becoming a mentor teacher. When the university began placing student teachers, Latoya reviewed the prospective student teachers' resumes and letters of introduction that were sent to her school. She chose two students she wanted to meet, and the university instructed the students to contact Latoya.

Latoya invited each prospective student teacher to spend time in her classroom. After an observation, each student talked with Latoya about her teaching practice and what the student hoped to experience and learn during student teaching. Latoya indicated on the university response form that she thought either student would work well in her classroom, adding, however, that she preferred the one whose view of good teaching was more like her own. The students, in turn, informed the student-teaching placement coordinator that they both wanted to work with Latoya. The placement coordinator looked at factors such as commuting distance for the students and comments from visits made to other teachers. She decided to place the student Latoya preferred with her. The other was placed with a more experienced mentor because of concerns about the student's progress.

Latoya met with her student teacher once more before the end of the school year to make plans for contact over the summer. Each expressed her enthusiasm for the coming fall, knowing that there would be much work ahead.

Vignette Dialogue Questions

1. Given the mentoring dispositions and beliefs described, why are all good teachers not necessarily good mentors?
2. What do you think about the ideas of "mutual consent" spelled out in the selection process used by Latoya and the prospective student teacher?
3. What administrative issues might arise in the development of such a model?
4. What can be done to minimize possible difficulties when a mentor requests a student teacher who specifically asks not to be placed with this mentor?

Induction Vignette
Mentoring Framework Dimension III: Mentor Selection and Mentor/Novice Matching at the Induction Level

Vignette Characters: School district personnel director and staff members.

Summary: It is important that a district develops guidelines for selecting mentor teachers and matching mentors with novice teachers. Selection criteria must be carefully aligned with program purposes for mentors to be agents of those purposes. Potential mentors will make informed decisions to participate if they have a full understanding of program requirements and expectations. The matching process must allow for regular communication between mentor and novice teacher.

Background and Context: For several years, 25 percent of the new teachers hired by the Metropolis school district (K–8) resigned their positions or were not selected for rehiring. The district's personnel office initiated a plan to determine the reasons for this loss and develop strategies for retaining new teachers in the future. Interviews and questionnaires completed by all teachers who had left the district suggested these common factors:

(1) feeling inadequately prepared to deal with the challenges they faced;
(2) feeling isolated, with little or no support from experienced colleagues;

(3) feeling overwhelmed by the complexities of the job; and

(4) lacking instructional resources and classroom materials.

Narrative: Formalizing a mentoring plan intended to improve teacher retention.

Using the results of their study of the previous year's new teachers, the district determined that a more formalized program of new-teacher support was needed. While each new teacher was assigned to an experienced "buddy" at his or her school site for initial orientation and was encouraged to participate in district in-service offerings, no other formalized programs of support for new teachers had previously existed.

The key component of that support would focus on a group of mentor teachers specifically trained using the knowledge base developed from current research and practice with induction-level teachers. Each mentor would then be assigned to work with and support several new teachers throughout the year.

Experienced teachers were invited to apply for the new teacher-mentor positions. The following qualifications were listed as selection factors:

(1) recommendations from administrators and colleagues regarding teaching performance;

(2) effective interpersonal communication skills;

(3) enthusiasm for teaching as a profession;

(4) evidence of a personal commitment to continued professional growth as a teacher; and

(5) previous successful experience in working with beginning teachers and/or student teachers.

A mentor-selection committee composed of the staff-development director, several administrators and experienced teachers, and two second-year teachers was identified. Interested applicants were invited to submit evidence of their performance in each of the five areas. After reviewing applicants' materials, the committee identified finalists for the positions, and the selection committee interviewed each of them.

During the interviews, candidates were asked if they were willing to participate in a week-long session to prepare for beginning mentoring responsibilities as well as continued professional-growth activities for mentors. It was agreed that those selected for mentor positions would receive a stipend for the five-day summer preparation workshop, ten days of release time to work with new teachers in their classrooms, and pay for any evening and/or Saturday meetings that were part of the program.

Based on the projected number and grade-level assignments of new hires, mentors were selected from primary, intermediate, and middle school levels. As new teachers were hired, they were assigned to an appropriate grade-level mentor. Whenever possible, the mentor was from the same school or one nearby that served a similar student population. The mentor teacher contacted the new teacher, made arrangements to meet at his or her school site, and offered assistance in preparing for the first days of the new school year.

A meeting and social function for all new teachers and mentors was held before school started. Each new teacher received a handbook of information that second-year teachers had identified as most useful and a calendar outlining the program activities throughout the year. A group of mentors and second- and third-year teachers role-played several scenarios of possible interactions to help new teachers understand the types of issues that could arise in the mentor–new teacher relationship throughout the year. Mentor teachers scheduled their first after-school conference with each new teacher to identify a focus area for assistance and support for the mentor's first scheduled classroom observation.

Vignette Dialogue Questions

1. What are the strengths and weaknesses of the mentor qualifications listed, and what deletions or additions would you suggest?
2. How might a local university with a teacher education undergraduate and graduate program be involved in this process?
3. How could the same quality level of mentor preparation be achieved in a district with very limited funding and with extreme difficulty in hiring sufficient numbers of substitutes?
4. How could these programming activities be strengthened?
5. When it is not possible to assign an on-site mentor, what strategies can facilitate quality mentoring?

NOTES

7

Mentor Preparation and Development (Mentoring Framework: Dimension IV)

by Sharon A. Schwille and Janet Dynak

DIMENSION ABSTRACT

The preparation of experienced teachers to assume the mentor role is key to quality mentoring programs. Experienced teachers must be sensitive to the types of knowledge, skills, and attitudes that foster professional growth for themselves and the novice teachers with whom they work. Mentors should be involved actively in professional-development work prior to and during their roles as mentors. Their work must be supported continually to develop their teaching and mentoring skills further. Mentors should examine and reflect on their own teaching practices as well as help novices learn to do so. Formal and ongoing professional development can provide the necessary foundation and structure for mentor growth. Moreover, the opportunity to work together to improve mentoring practices, instruction, and student learning will enable participants to move toward standards-based education with high expectations for both teachers and students.

Regularly scheduled meetings of mentor teachers can be helpful, providing opportunities to share ideas, successes, and problems. Mentors should be encouraged to discuss their views of good teaching and expectations of novices as they develop practices that demonstrate good teaching. At times, creative problem-solving sessions allow mentors to pool their collective wisdom of practice, helping one another with suggestions for dealing with particular challenges. Facilitators who are knowledgeable about mentoring practices and beginning-teacher learning can assist with these meetings, challenging mentors to think about the work of mentoring and helping novices learn to teach. In other words, such sessions can enhance mentors' own professional development. Similar meetings for novice teachers are also useful.

Every mentoring program must have a plan to provide incentives and rewards for mentors. The plan should address providing adequate time, recognition, and even additional compensation. In addition, mentors should participate in making decisions to identify and prioritize incentives and rewards.

COMPONENTS WITH INDICATORS OF QUALITY
Component IV.1: Initial Preparation and Ongoing Professional Development

- Mentors actively participate in intensive preparation prior to beginning a mentoring assignment.
- Mentors actively participate in ongoing, formal professional development related to mentoring and learning standards-based teaching practice.

Component IV.2: Content of Professional Development

Mentor professional development focuses on, but is not limited to:

- observing and analyzing the practice of novices, with emphasis on professional standards-based teaching;
- national and local reform initiatives to enhance teaching;
- collecting classroom data;
- communicating and resolving conflict;
- understanding novice development and the needs/concerns of novices;
- fostering productive conversations about teaching and learning;
- studying the mentor's own teaching and helping the novice learn from these processes;
- analyzing the learning of diverse students and helping the novice learn from these processes;
- mentoring strategies and practices to support and challenge

novices to learn at their maximal level;
- analyzing school and district contexts and their influence on mentoring, teaching, and learning to teach;
- working with novices as adult learners; and
- exploring ways to facilitate the novice's use of school, district, and community resources.

Component IV.3: Professional-Development Activities

Mentors will:
- reflect on their own experiences as novices;
- practice and problem solve simulated and/or actual mentor/ novice learning situations; *Case Studies*
- analyze and reflect on classroom teaching and learning experiences as well as mentor/novice interactions;
- receive coaching and feedback on mentoring practices;
- share and study mentoring practices with other mentors; and
- explore strategies to build and strengthen the mentor/novice relationship.

Component IV.4: Mentor Incentives for Professional Development

- The program provides mentors with time for mentor professional development during contract days of the school year; and/or
- The program provides mentors with monetary compensation for attending mentoring-related professional development conducted outside the contract day; and/or
- Credit earned through mentor professional development may be used for advancement on school district salary schedule, certificate-renewal requirements, and/or university degree work.

DISCUSSION QUESTIONS

1. Is the initial preparation of mentors sufficient to help them meet the immediate challenges of assisting the novice teacher and develop understanding and ownership of the broader, long-range purposes of the program? What improvements can be made in the existing initial preparation of mentor teachers?

2. What opportunities do mentors have to practice and solve simu-

lated and actual problems related to mentoring? Do current preparation and development activities rely too heavily on "telling" mentors how to mentor rather than engaging them in productive conversations about mentoring? How can professional-development activities be modified to engage mentors more?

3. How well do preparation and development activities for mentors help them focus on the goal of helping novice teachers develop standards-based teaching practices? What revisions or additions can be made in preparation and professional-development activities to facilitate this type of support?

4. What ongoing professional-development activities exist to help mentors learn more about mentoring and teaching? What additional activities can be initiated to facilitate mentors' continuous growth and learning?

5. Are current mentor incentives, rewards, and/or compensation sufficient to support program purposes? What additional incentives and rewards can be provided, and what is the plan for doing so?

COMMON PROBLEMS

- Mentors receive professional development only at the beginning of the school year.
- Mentor professional development does not include the perspective of professional standards-based teaching.
- Mentors receive inadequate incentives and/or compensation for time devoted to professional development.
- Mentors are provided with minimal preparation or opportunity for professional development.
- Professional development is not grounded in research on effective practice.
- A facilitator with limited knowledge or experience in the field of mentoring or ineffective presentation skills provides the training.

VIGNETTES

Preservice Vignette
Mentoring Framework Dimension IV: Mentor
Preparation and Development at the Preservice Level

Vignette Characters: Becky, a mentor of preservice novices, and several colleagues.

Summary: Like teaching, mentoring is a professional practice that must be learned and continually developed through opportunities for professional growth. Good mentoring requires a diversity of support structures, such as frequent interaction among mentors, institutes in which mentoring and its forms of practice are studied, and university courses geared toward mentors' learning. Mentor-teacher learning and professional development happens over time and is recognized by appropriate incentives.

Background and Context: Becky, an experienced teacher and mentor of student teachers, volunteered to help plan the mentor-teacher professional-development institutes sponsored by the university for the next school year. She took the university's course for mentors as part of her own learning experience. She continued to develop her understanding and enactment of mentoring by participating in mentor-teaching professional-development groups and institutes over the years that she was a mentor. As a step in stretching her own thinking about mentor professional development, she wanted to participate in planning and leading opportunities for her mentor colleagues' development.

Narrative: Opportunities for mentor-teacher preparation and professional development.

On her way to the planning meeting for the summer institute for mentor teachers, Becky thought about what she considered important for a mentor teacher to learn. As an experienced mentor of preservice teachers, she knew that learning to mentor takes time and willingness to examine one's own practice as well as helping student teachers learn to examine theirs. She thought the summer institute needed to address mentoring purposes and clarify the role of mentors as educational companions. Though she realized that some time must be devoted to looking at schedules, procedures, and evaluation forms for the student teachers, she wanted to advocate that most of the institute time be devoted to helping mentors learn more about the practice of mentoring and the many forms that it takes to help novices effectively learn to teach.

Becky knew from her own experience at these institutes that mentors especially appreciate sessions that help them think about ways to work with their student teachers. These sessions, which incorporate small-group discussions with other mentors and often a university teacher educator, focus on key aspects of working effectively with novices, such as engaging in co-planning, co-teaching, and facilitating reflective conversations about both the mentor's and the student teacher's teaching. The sessions also address issues of building constructive working relationships between mentors and novices and understanding what student teachers must learn as they begin their professional careers. Several sessions focus on teaching subject matter according to current reform-minded, standards-based practice. Becky thought these sessions help push mentors' thinking about teaching and learning as well as help them understand what student teachers are expected to try during their student teaching. The summer institute is usually two weeks before school starts, which has helped Becky prepare for the new school year. It normally lasts 2-1/2 days, with the student teachers attending the last half-day session. Becky liked this structured time with her student teacher to discuss how they envisioned their work together.

As Becky arrived at the planning meeting, she greeted several of her mentor and university colleagues from the past couple of years. They had been through many lively and challenging discussions together as part of their mentor professional-development program sponsored by the university. They now felt like trusted professional colleagues. They joked about how quickly the summer had passed, adding that no one was ready for school to begin. The group decided to present a new videotape from the institute, showing a mentor and student teacher working together. From their preview of the tape, they thought it would generate rich discussions about the work of mentoring and how people learn to teach. Seeing aspects of mentoring in action such as coaching, co-planning, reflective conferencing, and writing journals, the mentors could visualize and discuss their roles and responsibilities.

Becky knew the mentors would appreciate the small stipend they received for attending the institute. The stipend payment was a shared responsibility of the university and the school district, because each has an investment in teachers' professional development. In past years, Becky used hers to purchase materials that she would otherwise not have for her classroom. This year, she looked forward to attending a conference, using the stipend to pay the registration fee. In addition, the university and school district contributed to a professional fund that allows mentors to have a substitute teacher on occasion so that they can spend time with their student teachers away from the classroom. They could even use the time to observe other mentors working with their student teachers. This arrangement would ease some of the time pressures that teachers experience. Becky made a mental note to plan for some of this substitute time before the year got too stressful.

On her drive home, Becky switched her thinking to the year ahead. She had already reserved alternate Tuesday afternoons after school for mentor group meetings. This small group of mentors, from her own school and a school nearby, would meet to continue the conversations on mentoring practice that began at the summer institute. The university professor who acts as the student teachers' field instructor also would attend the mentor-group sessions. Becky values these conversations with colleagues because they support her professional development both as a mentor and teacher.

Vignette Dialogue Questions

1. What kind of time commitment is necessary for a mentor like Becky, and what kinds of administrative support are necessary to make it a successful experience?
2. What kinds of activities and topics could the mentor group address in their work with the university supervisor?
3. What do mentors need to understand about teacher development to have realistic expectations of student teachers?
4. How might Becky's relationship with her student teacher affect the students they share in class?

Induction Vignette
Mentoring Framework Dimension IV: Mentor Preparation and Development at the Induction Level

Vignette Character: Mario, a mentor of induction-level beginning teachers.

Summary: Mentors of induction-level teachers need initial preparation and continuing professional development to gain knowledge and expertise in mentoring as a professional practice. This preparation and development should take a variety of forms and occur over time. It should support mentors' intellectual and pedagogical growth both as mentors and classroom teachers. Appropriate incentives for mentors are a fundamental component of an effective program.

Background and Context: Mario, an experienced classroom teacher, applied for a mentoring position in his district. In a moderately sized city, his district hires about 75 new teachers every year. He wanted to be a mentor because he believed that beginning teachers should be supported during their early years and not have to endure the "sink or swim" approach of learning to teach like he did. He knew being a mentor meant that he needed initial preparation for the role and continued professional development in order to learn the practice.

Narrative: A mentor-preparation session.

Honored by his acceptance as a mentor for new teachers in his school district, Mario looked forward to the preparation institute offered for mentor teachers by the district for one week during the summer. Mario knew he had teaching expertise to draw upon to help beginning teachers get off to a good start, but he also realized that he needed to learn how to mentor effectively. In a sense, he felt like a new teacher too, but the "subject matter" he needed to learn involved helping novices learn to teach rather than academic subject matter.

Looking over the agenda for the institute, Mario noticed that each day had a focus—adults as learners, forms of mentoring, building relationships, and engaging in constructive interpersonal interactions. The opening day would begin with a keynote speaker who would talk about the importance of mentoring induction-year teachers and the knowledge base mentors need to work effectively. Mario recognized this speaker as someone very knowledgeable about research on teacher induction and mentoring as well as an experienced mentor herself. Her talk would be both intellectually stimulating and relevant to practice. The district administrator who coordinates the mentoring program would present the district's philosophy or stance toward mentoring as a professional practice and explain the district's

policies and procedures related to the mentoring program. Other sessions during the week would include looking at national and state curriculum standards and what it means to help a novice teacher shape his or her practice to align with those standards.

Much of the summer institute time would be spent in small-group discussions about mentors' roles and practices. Panels of experienced mentors talking about their practice, videotapes of mentor/novice pairs in action, role plays of mentor/novice interactions, and vignettes of dilemmas and problems of practice would provide bases for conversations to help mentors examine their own assumptions, beliefs, and questions about mentoring and learning to teach. Some sessions would be for new mentors only, so that they could begin to explore issues and questions of practice that the more experienced mentors have already encountered. Meanwhile, the experienced mentors would be in their own sessions, focusing on intricacies and refinements of mentoring practices. Each of these sessions would push the participants' thinking at their particular levels of mentor development.

Mario knew that the summer institute would be the beginning of a yearlong program including meetings with fellow mentors twice a month. Experienced mentors would lead the group. The conversations would focus on mentors' current work with their novices as well as their own teaching practices. About three times during the year, the district would sponsor one-day institutes for the mentors focusing on standards-based teaching, learning, and learning to teach. Experts would present sessions focused on subject matter so mentors could further examine teaching toward standards-based curriculum and practice.

Mario was pleased to be selected as a mentor in his district because it signified that he was considered a good teaching model as well as a good teacher educator. He had the option of receiving a stipend for the meetings and institutes he attended outside the school contract day or applying for credit toward the state-required educational units needed to maintain his certification. He was released from classroom teaching for a portion of each week to perform his mentoring responsibilities. He looked forward to his new role and its challenges as a way to continue his own professional development and explore his fascination with teaching and learning—not only in his classroom but also with novices in theirs.

Vignette Dialogue Questions

1. Imagine Mario encounters a novice teacher with a view of good teaching that differs greatly from Mario's. He is not sure how to handle this situation. What resources could help him learn how to address such a problem?

2. How might Mario share ways he employs standards-based teaching with other mentors and novice teachers?

3. What are some of the issues Mario may face balancing his mentor responsibilities with other school and district professional responsibilities?

4. What mentor-development activities could be included in the one-day institutes to prepare mentors better to assist novices with their emotional and instructional concerns?

5. In addition to participating in mentor-development activities, what else can Mario do to prepare himself to deal with his novice's struggles with the realities of beginning teaching?

8

Mentor Roles and Practices (Mentoring Framework: Dimension V)

by Janet Dynak and Gary P. DeBolt

DIMENSION ABSTRACT

The roles of mentors and their practices are at the heart of quality mentoring programs. High-quality mentors view themselves as instructional leaders and as teacher educators continuing to grow professionally themselves. Mentoring roles are multifaceted and demanding; yet successful mentors have positive attitudes toward the importance of their work. They view their roles as facilitators of the professional growth of novices, maintaining their focus on instructional improvement.

Mentors must be active learners; they must be positive and reflective throughout their work with novice teachers. The work of the mentor/novice pair should center on support, challenge, guidance, and development. In addition, mentoring practices should be consistent with the overall purposes of the program. Program planners should assist the pair in assessing needs and progress. Each pair will develop unique characteristics and ways of working together—a natural and expected outcome of the relationship.

COMPONENTS WITH INDICATORS OF QUALITY
Component V.1: Mentor's View of Role and Relationship to Novice

- The mentor perceives himself or herself as a school-based teacher educator, taking responsibility for supporting, facilitating, and challenging novices into standards-based practice.

- The mentor views his or her role as a facilitator and model of self-reflection, problem-solving, and instructional improvement.
- The mentor consistently recognizes trustworthiness and professional growth as the defining dimensions of the mentor/novice relationship.
- The mentor accepts the ongoing responsibility of building and maintaining a professional relationship with the novice.

Component V.2: Mentor-Teacher Participation in Preparation and Ongoing Development

- The mentor actively participates in and pursues opportunities for professional growth *in mentoring.*
- The mentor actively pursues individual and collaborative opportunities for professional growth *in teaching.*
- The mentor actively pursues opportunities to communicate with faculty members from universities to study research-based knowledge about learning to teach.
- Experienced mentors assist in the preparation of new mentors.

Component V.3: Focus of Mentor/Novice Work

- The mentor provides initial support and guidance to the novice before school begins and continues with frequent and regular interaction throughout the school year.
- The mentor and novice cooperatively and intentionally develop and maintain a focus for their work together rooted in standards-based teaching practice.
- The mentor supports and challenges the novice to improve his or her teaching practices.
- The mentor/novice collaborative work involves a variety of professional-development experiences—observations of one another, collaborative planning and teaching, journaling—targeted at ongoing instructional improvement.
- The mentor/novice work is dynamic; it is based on and informed by formative assessment of particular novice needs and a shared understanding of standards-based teaching practice.
- Interactions between mentor and novice are both formal and informal, occurring in and out of the mentor's and/or novice's classroom.

- The mentor provides empathy and assistance to novices coping with the stresses of teaching.

DISCUSSION QUESTIONS

1. To what degree do mentors perceive themselves as responsible for helping novice teachers learn to teach? In what ways do mentor teachers support and challenge novices as they learn standards-based practice? In what ways are mentors able to guide novice teachers in the pursuit of standards-based teaching practices? In their work with novices, do some mentors find that they deal primarily with management issues or social interactions? What steps can be taken to elevate the work of the mentor/novice pair?

2. In what ways do mentors develop and maintain a trusting relationship with novice teachers? When mentors find themselves struggling with confidentiality and trust issues, what are the best ways of dealing with these sensitive issues? If the mentor/novice match is not working well, what procedures are in place to assist and/or change the situation?

3. To what degree is the focus of the mentor/novice work determined collaboratively? How can mentors encourage novice teachers to identify for themselves areas of teaching on which they must focus? What activities can promote collaborative identification of focus areas?

4. What evidence is there that mentors are sensitive to teaching-related emotional stress that novices experience? Do mentors consistently provide caring and productive responses in helping novices learn to teach? What activities can increase mentors' awareness of the importance of addressing novice teachers' emotional needs while also maintaining a focus on instructional improvement?

5. To what degree do mentors find that they become critical or negative of novice teachers who exhibit less than favorable attitudes and/or behaviors? What can be done to encourage novices to improve? How can mentors be supported and encouraged in these circumstances?

COMMON PROBLEMS

- The mentor views his or her role as dispenser of information and advice when time permits.

- The mentor relies on the novice to initiate, build, and maintain a relationship, relying on the novice to seek assistance rather than accepting the responsibility for ongoing support.
- The mentor has not adjusted his or her schedule to allow for the time commitment necessary for quality mentoring.
- The mentor addresses too many issues simultaneously with novice.
- The mentor attempts to focus the pair's work without giving the novice voice in the decision-making process.
- The mentor and novice focus their work around only day-to-day situations and problems encountered.
- The mentor acknowledges emotional needs of the novice but provides limited help only in problem solving and improving instruction.
- The mentor functions as a conditional helper dependent upon the novice's attitude, behavior, or performance and becomes negative and critical when novice does not measure up to mentor's expectations.

VIGNETTES

Preservice Vignette
Mentoring Framework Dimension V:
Mentor Roles and Practices at the Preservice Level

Vignette Characters: Karen, a mentor, and Tom, her student teacher.

Summary: It is important during their first few meetings that the mentor and novice teacher together establish that the mentor's role is one of a facilitator promoting self-reflection and problem solving. The focus of work is cooperatively and intentionally developed to improve teaching quality and the learning experiences of students. The mentor's support and guidance is caring and helpful on a regularly scheduled basis.

Background and Context: In early June, Karen, an experienced middle school teacher and mentor, read the autobiographical sketch written by Tom, who was to be her fall student teacher. Before the school year ended, Tom had observed in Karen's classroom, and she gave him some texts and curriculum materials to guide his preparation work over the summer. They set up a series of planning sessions during August.

Narrative: First planning session.

At the first planning session in August, Karen asked Tom what he thought her role as mentor should be. Tom replied that he felt she should serve as a model and that he would observe her, eventually taking over some of the instruction. Karen explained that, while modeling is part of her role, she saw herself supporting and guiding him—and that, from the beginning of the year, they would collaboratively decide on instructional practices.

The two of them discussed how the classroom environment could be created. Karen probed Tom with questions such as: "How do you think we could show the students we are a team?" "Do you have any additional ideas for activities to get to know the students and their interests?" Tom described an introduction activity that he had used to learn students' names during an earlier field experience. In the activity, the student gives an adjective beginning with the same letter as the student's first name that describes one of his or her personality traits. "Tumbling Tina," for example, was the student who took gymnastic lessons and hoped to get really good at it. Karen suggested that they use the activity on the first day, because many students were coming from feeder elementary schools and wouldn't know one another.

Later, they talked about the instructional process as it related to planning, implementing, and monitoring lessons. Karen asked Tom to think about and share with her areas in which he was knowledgeable and those in which he believed he would need more support and guidance. Tom explained that he usually had a lot of good ideas about planning units of study activities. He also stated that he was comfortable working with small groups of students, but that he had difficulty with whole-group instruction. Karen suggested that they could co-teach initially, with Tom doing most of the planning while she would lead the whole-group implementation. Karen suggested, then, that Tom could complement her whole-group instruction with examples and further exploration of concepts and that he could facilitate any small-group work that they would use.

Near the end of the meeting, Karen discussed methods that they could use for reflection together in the little planning time scheduled each day. She told Tom how she and a previous student teacher wrote journal entries to each other a couple of times per week because she had to coach right after school. She explained that she wanted to establish some regular form of reflection and asked for his suggestions. By that point in their conversation, Karen had shown Tom that she had been listening to him and that she was using his feedback to make decisions about how they would work together. Therefore, Tom felt comfortable sharing that he did not really like writing journals and has had to do many of them in university classes. Also, he would have to do one each week for his student teaching seminar. They brainstormed other ways to communicate regularly without the interruptions common to a school day and discovered that they both liked to stay up late at night. That discovery led them to set up weekly phone conferences at 10 P.M. on Wednesdays. In addition, they planned two more meetings to organize the first units of study.

Vignette Dialogue Questions

1. In what ways did Karen encourage Tom to contribute his ideas at their first meeting? What other means would encourage novices to share at initial meetings with their mentors?
2. What are future plans or issues that Karen and Tom may wish to consider?
3. What are some ways that Karen may transition Tom gradually into more teaching responsibilities over the semester?
4. In addition to the formal mentoring program, what additional resources might Karen access to support her work with Tom?
5. In what other ways might Karen increase her communication with Tom?

Induction Vignette
Mentoring Framework Dimension V:
Mentor Roles and Practices at the Induction Level

Vignette Characters: Harvey, a mentor teacher, and Carla, a novice teacher.

Summary: The mentor facilitates self-reflection and problem solving with the novice teacher. By demonstrating a willingness to take risks and seek feedback, a trusting relationship can be established. The mentor and novice must interact often and cooperatively. They must intentionally focus their work together on quality teaching and learning experiences for their students.

Background and Context: Carla has just completed her first month of teaching math at the high school level. As her mentor and colleague in the math department, Harvey met regularly with Carla—two to three times per week—during their common planning period. Carla feels comfortable asking Harvey for support and soliciting suggestions from him about creating a positive classroom environment for the five groups of students that she teaches each day. During the last week, their conversations focused on one group of students that Carla perceives to be less motivated than are students in the other classes. At one point, Carla told Harvey that she was exhausted from trying to get them to participate in class discussions and group work. Harvey listened to Carla, knowing it was important, but knew that he must help Carla find different instructional approaches for those students.

Narrative: Mentoring in action.

Harvey reflected upon how he could assist Carla with her struggle to motivate her fifth-hour students. From his mentor preparation and the district mentor program, Harvey knew that could get release time to observe Carla teaching. In addition, he thought specifically about the motivation level of that class and formulated a co-teaching idea that he believed might help them both develop better instructional strategies to elicit more student participation.

At their next meeting, Harvey suggested that they plan an observation of Carla's fifth-hour class followed by a co-teaching experience, explaining that it would benefit them both. Carla agreed but asked Harvey to observe, also, a class in which her teaching had been more effective.

To provide a focus for the observations, Harvey asked Carla to identify a specific part of the instructional process about which she wanted feedback. In her second-hour class—the one she believed had the most positive classroom environment—Carla had been consciously working on questioning techniques to probe students' prior knowledge. In addition, students in the second-hour class were working through problems, rather than reviewing the complete problem-solving method, when they asked for assistance. The fifth-hour class, however, participated little and seldom sought assistance on concepts and problems. Carla wanted help with methods that would encourage participation from these students.

Harvey took notes, concentrating on their predetermined focus area, during two observations the week following their conversation. When he and Carla met after school to discuss the observations, Harvey complimented Carla on her knowledge of content and her ability to engage the students in the second-hour class. He acknowledged her attempts to link the steps of a given problem to students' prior knowledge, offering a few suggestions to strengthen that process. He recommended she draw upon students' common knowledge, such as basketball, to link lessons to prior knowledge.

As for the fifth-hour class, Harvey told Carla that the students must expect to be called upon. The students could have the option to pass, he told her, but they should be called on to answer questions or give feedback. He shared that fielding could alternate between random selection and seating order to increase expectations and awareness. Occasionally, Carla should let the students know that a certain subject would be discussed the following day to give students time to prepare. Harvey added that these experiences might help the students become more comfortable volunteering, something his own fifth-hour class needed.

Carla mentioned that they had talked earlier about co-teaching to try more effective discussion strategies. Harvey nodded, suggesting they try parallel teaching with their fifth-hour classes. In this form of co-teaching, they would each teach their own class, but they would use the same strategies and then reflect together about their use. They planned to introduce the new participation ideas—random, seating-order, and forecasted—to their classes on the following Monday. Once the ideas were introduced and begun, Harvey and Carla planned to meet informally to discuss progress, with a formal meeting for reflection at the end of the week.

Vignette Dialogue Questions

1. How is the relationship between Carla and Harvey reciprocal?

2. In what ways did Harvey provide learning opportunities for Carla while realizing some that he could use? How does a mentor decide what forms of mentoring are most appropriate for a novice?
3. What other concerns might Carla have at this point in her teaching in addition to the difficulties with her fifth-hour class?
4. How might Harvey facilitate Carla's problem-solving abilities and exploration of other resources to help address her classroom challenges?

NOTES

9
Program Administration, Implementation, and Evaluation (Mentoring Framework: Dimension VI)

by Alan J. Reiman and Janet Dynak

DIMENSION ABSTRACT

Program administration, implementation, and evaluation tie an effective mentoring program together. Planning a program must include the best provision of leadership. Choosing good leaders, establishing a decision-making process, and implementing and evaluating program goals and objectives are essential in creating a mentoring program.

When selecting the program coordinator, participants should help develop the criteria desired in a candidate. The candidate accepting the role must have clearly defined responsibilities and adequate support—financial and personal—for successful program implementation. The administration of the school and the college or university involved should make decisions consistent with program purposes.

In developing mentoring programs—whether for preservice teachers or in-service novices—planners must consider the complex web of relationships existing across the six dimensions of quality mentoring outlined in this volume. We hope that these dimensions provide a useful framework for planning, implementing, and continually evaluating mentoring programs.

COMPONENTS WITH INDICATORS OF QUALITY
Component VI.1: Program-Coordinator Criteria and Assignment

The program coordinator:

- is committed to program purposes;
- is knowledgeable and experienced in mentoring initiatives;
- has administrative authority and expertise to coordinate university and school involvement in the mentoring program;
- has a substantial portion or all of his or her job assignment devoted to the mentor program; and
- is able to work effectively with people of diverse backgrounds.

Component VI.2: Program-Coordinator Responsibility

The program coordinator:

- arranges incentives for mentors;
- facilitates the process of selecting mentors and matching them with novices;
- coordinates professional development for mentors and novices;
- facilitates efforts between the school, teacher unions, district, and university to support mentor and novice professional development;
- coordinates program research and evaluation efforts; and
- works with program participants to schedule time for mentors to carry out mentoring responsibilities and study mentoring practices.

Component VI.3: Program Evaluation

- Evaluation addresses program purposes including the novice's learning and teaching practice, effectiveness of mentoring practices, teacher retention and certification, and effectiveness of program activities.
- Evaluation is designed collaboratively by a representative group of program participants—school district personnel, university faculty, etc.
- Data are collected continuously from a wide variety of stakeholders including mentors, novices, administrators, and others.
- Formative and summative evaluation data are collected,

shared, and used throughout the year. Results are continually analyzed and provide guidance for program modification and refinement.

DISCUSSION QUESTIONS

1. How is policy determined?
2. In what ways is the administration and coordination of the program given priority and support? To what degree is program coordination assigned as "one more task" to those who are already overloaded with other job demands? What can be done to enhance program coordination?
3. How is the program supported by ongoing coordination activities? To what degree is the program expected to "run itself" once mentor and novice pairing and initial mentor preparation has been completed? What ongoing coordination needs exist, and how can these needs best be addressed?
4. In what ways is program evaluation approached as an ongoing part of program implementation? To what degree is evaluation approached as an afterthought or as a necessary but undesirable program task? What can be done to enhance program-evaluation efforts?

COMMON PROBLEMS

*   No one oversees the program after the initial preparation of mentors, and no one follows up on program maintenance or adjustments.
*   Program administration is assigned as "one more task" to a person or governing body having too many other competing demands, limited ownership of the mentoring programs, and/or little expertise or experience in mentoring.
*   Mentors receive inadequate compensation, praise, or recognition for their participation in the program.
*   Inadequate release and planning time is allowed for the mentor and novice to work together.
*   Little or no program evaluation occurs, or evaluation is limited to participant-satisfaction ratings or attendance at meetings.
*   Evaluation is designed with little or no input from stakeholders and does not specifically address program goals, or it is de-

signed primarily to meet external evaluation requirements.
- Evaluation data are not gathered on an ongoing basis; instead, data are gathered at the beginning and end of the school year.
- A formal structure facilitating interaction among all stakeholders to formulate policy is not in place.

VIGNETTES

Preservice Vignette
Mentoring Framework Dimension VI: Program Administration, Implementation, and Evaluation at the Preservice Level

Vignette Characters: University faculty members and selected classroom teacher leaders identified to become school-based teacher educators.

Summary: The implementation and evaluation of a mentoring program should be linked to the core values, mission statements, and strategic goals that have been collectively established by teachers and teacher organizations, policy makers, and faculty members from colleges and universities. A representative group may implement the program and assess the program outcomes.

Background and Context: Representative faculty and administration from a university joined selected teachers and administrators from a large school district to implement and evaluate an improved preservice teacher education program that featured a state-of-the-art professional-development program for exemplary teachers to serve as school-based teacher educators. The program plan stated that, after a yearlong professional-development program for teams of teacher leaders, the teacher leaders would, in turn, provide professional development to prospective mentors of preservice teachers in specific schools. This vignette highlights efforts of this tiered professional-development plan.

Narrative: Summary of the first year of program implementation and evaluation.

During the first year, university faculty members and selected teacher leaders met in weekly three-hour sessions to read and discuss benchmark skills as well as background theory and research in teacher education, mentoring, teacher development, coaching, and assistance. Activities were designed so that teacher leaders could practice skills in their school setting following each seminar meeting. For example, each teacher leader audiotaped a conference with a colleague in which they modeled effective listening skills. During the spring, the teacher leaders were assigned a preservice teacher, who worked with them in their classrooms. Through the use of videotapes and audiotapes, they self-assessed their mentoring skills and met together to discuss their work. This program phase was evaluated successfully by measured changes in the teacher leaders' use of mentoring skills, end-of-program evaluation, and by identification of resources for implementation in the school system. Such resources might include stipends for teacher leaders, preparation of curriculum for implementation, and professional release time for prospective mentors who would attend school-based programs.

The initial evaluation established a need for the development of a field manual that was then designed by the teacher leaders identified as school-based teacher educators and university faculty. The manual included information on benchmark activities and resources that could be used by the mentor or preservice teacher. Topics covered in the manual were: building a helping relationship; roles and expectations; instructional planning; coaching and clinical assistance; promoting preservice teacher learning and development; documentation; and standards-based assessment.

When the year ended, the school-based teacher educators met with school system personnel and university faculty members to plan for the implementation of the same professional-development program in their school system. The goal was to implement six school-based teacher sites using the curriculum they developed with the university faculty that year. A timeline for the following year's activities was established. During the fall, it was decided that the school-based teacher educators would provide weekly professional development for the prospective mentors at the six sites. In the winter, each mentor would be assigned a student teacher and continue the weekly professional-development meetings. Student teachers would meet weekly in a seminar co-taught by the school-based teacher educators.

Before adjourning for summer break, school-based teacher educators and assigned university faculty members from the six sites outlined an ongoing formative and summative evaluation for the following year. The outlines called for participants to document their learning and teaching practices as well as the effectiveness of mentoring practices and program activities. All participants would provide feedback about their experiences through case studies. Monthly meetings to review the case study reports and make appropriate program changes were scheduled.

Vignette Dialogue Questions

1. In what ways can a field manual address the need to link mentoring with standards-based teaching?
2. How much time commitment is needed for this plan, and how can that time be made available to participants?
3. How might this partnership affect the mentors' teaching practices in their own classrooms?
4. How could a national board-certified teacher's expertise help this type of program?
5. By what means can a participant's ability to balance teaching responsibilities with requests for evaluation data and case studies be monitored?
6. How can information from monthly meetings be communicated back to program administrators, other policy makers, and stakeholders?

Induction Vignette
Mentoring Framework Dimension VI: Program Administration, Implementation, and Evaluation at the Induction Level

Vignette Characters: A director of professional development, a coordinator for school and university programs, and two school-based teacher educators.

Summary: The implementation and evaluation of a mentoring program for beginning teachers should be linked to program purposes that have been collaboratively developed by the school system, teachers and teacher organizations, policy makers, and university faculty members. A representative group, then, collaboratively implements the program and assesses program outcomes.

Background and Context: Representative faculty members and administrators from a university joined the director of professional development and two school-based teacher educators (lead mentors) from a large school district to implement and evaluate an improved induction program for novice professionals. The program featured a state-of-the-art professional-development program for teachers as school-based teacher educators. The task for this group was to develop a professional-support program that seamlessly connected preservice teacher education with induction and ongoing professional development. This vignette highlights selected efforts of the team as they implemented and evaluated the program.

Narrative: Summary of three years of implementation.

After considerable study and review of teacher-development literature and research, the facilitating team agreed to adopt goals that were first proposed by Griffin (1985). These goals were to:

- link preservice support, induction, and ongoing professional development;
- emphasize support, not screening, for beginning professionals;
- prepare mentors who are highly skilled in assisting and coaching preservice and beginning educators;
- provide a quality orientation to the community, school system, school, and classroom;
- support professional release time for beginning professionals and mentors;
- communicate goals of the program to all building administrators and school staff members;
- provide ongoing opportunities for beginning educators to discuss concerns together in a setting free of evaluation; and
- provide a reduced teaching assignment for beginning educators.

Over the next three years, the school system and partner university developed an ongoing, yearlong professional-development program for prospective mentors of preservice and beginning educators. The program supported beginning teachers, counselors, and school psychologists. As well, the school system developed a week-long orientation for all beginning educators.

During the second year of the program, biweekly support seminars led by teacher and counselor facilitators were sponsored for beginning educators, and the school system provided five days of professional release time for each mentee and mentor. Furthermore, all building-level administrators were informed about the importance of supporting new professionals within the school system. Ongoing reflection and portfolio development were built into the program.

During the third year of the program, a summer institute was developed to update skills for mentors. However, no formalized program was put in place to reduce first- and second-year teachers' assignments.

Careful articulation of program goals allowed ongoing assessment and evaluation of goals. At the end of the third year, all goals but one had been reached. The facilitating team began planning for more rigorous evaluations that included exit interviews with the departing beginning educators, case-study analyses of highly successful mentor and beginning educator teams, as well as more rigorous mentor-selection procedures.

Vignette Dialogue Questions

1. How were program goals actualized in this program?
2. What program refinements and improvements were made in the second and third years of the program?
3. What is the value of identifying program goals at the beginning of the program-development process? How often should program goals be revisited and revised?
4. The final goal—reduced teaching assignments for novice teachers—was not achieved. What are some possible reasons for this failing? What strategies might allow program leaders to advance and attain that goal?
5. What additional goals may be considered for program improvement?
6. What questions might be important to include in novice teachers' exit interviews?

REFERENCE

Griffin, G. A. 1985. Teacher induction: Research issues. *Journal of Teacher Education* 36(1): 42–6.

Section III

The Mentoring Framework—
A National Perspective

10

A Survey of the 50 States: Mandated Teacher-Induction Programs

by Barry W. Sweeny and Gary P. DeBolt

With this book, the Association of Teacher Educators (ATE) and Kappa Delta Pi (KDP) take a significant step beyond previous work to capture and share the knowledge base for effective mentoring programs and practices. The Mentoring Framework provides a comprehensive guide for mentor programming and mentoring practice. It incorporates practitioner wisdom gained from working with many programs from inception through implementation, including many cycles of evaluation and revision. Application of the Mentoring Framework, however, cannot take place in isolation. Local mentoring programs exist within a state context, including whatever mandates and policies guide local practice. This chapter provides the induction context for each of the 50 states and the District of Columbia. It also offers guidance for using the Mentoring Framework to improve the effectiveness of both state and local mentoring programs and practices.

BACKGROUND

In 1997 and 1998, the Teacher Induction Advisory Group for the Illinois State Board of Education was charged with recommending how to implement a state-mandated induction-program model and standards for teachers. An interest in factors related to induction-program success led to a survey of the induction programs in all 50 states and the District of Columbia. The group was also interested in knowing how much assistance and support to novice teachers state programs were providing and if they were focusing on assessment of novice teachers' knowledge and skills.

Comparing several earlier surveys and analyses of state induction programs (American Federation of Teachers 1998; Barger 1986; Consortium for Policy Research in Education 1996; Defino and Hoffman 1984; Elias, McDonald, Stevenson, Simon, and Fisher 1980; Elias, McDonald, and Simon 1980; Furtwengler 1993; Hawk and Robards 1987; Hoffman, Edwards, Paulissen, O'Neal, and Barnes 1985; McDonald 1980a; McDonald 1980b; Neuweiler 1988; Sclan and Darling-Hammond 1992; Simon 1980), a confusing picture surfaced, with programs appearing and disappearing over time. No consistent pattern of improvement or development was evident across the states. At the time, there was no current survey that sufficiently analyzed the assistance or assessment approaches of the 50 states. Sweeny (1998) decided to conduct a state review, draw conclusions about the assistance-versus-assessment issues, and make the results accessible on a Web site. In 1998, this state-survey project was deemed relevant to the work of the ATE/KDP Commission on the Professional Support and Development for Novice Teachers. Accordingly, it is reported here. In addition, readers are encouraged to access the extensive report of a national study of urban teacher-induction programs and practices entitled *Learning the Ropes* (Fideler and Haselkorn 1999).

METHODOLOGY

When the ATE/KDP Commission adopted the state-survey project, we checked the information for accuracy and timeliness. In May 1998, each state department was asked a common set of questions regarding its induction programs. The questions included whether or not states mandated mentoring of novices and, if so, asked for a description of the mandate. The states were also queried about when mentoring programs were established; what the primary purposes were; who was required to be involved; what support, resources, and training were provided for those involved; and how they defined the role of the mentor. The state representatives also were asked to share additional information about their induction programs in narrative form. The survey included the original state program information from the Web site. In all, 36 states responded to the survey, a return rate of about 72 percent.

FINDINGS

As of August 1998, 28 states reported having current state-mandated teacher-induction programs. Of these programs, 26 provide a specifically targeted form of financial support, either in the form of competitive grants, Goals 2000 grants, staff-development money, or legislated appropriations (16 states). California, for example, has funded their Beginning Teacher Support and Assessment (BTSA) Program for several years for approximately 35 percent of new teachers. During 1998, the state legislature affirmed the cost-effectiveness of mentoring and increased the funding for the BTSA Program to address the needs of about 70 percent of California's beginning teachers.

Two states mandate induction programs but do not provide funding support. The New Jersey Teacher Induction Program provides no state money to support its mentoring program, which is for provisionally licensed teachers. They must pay $2,000 to support their own mentoring. So, in the New Jersey case, there is support for a mandated program, but it is not state funded.

STATE PROGRAM PILOTS

Eleven states currently do not have statewide teacher-induction programs but sponsor, intend to sponsor, or have sponsored pilot programs in the past. These include Alabama, Illinois, Maryland, Massachusetts, Minnesota, Montana, New Hampshire, North Dakota, Texas, Virginia, and Wisconsin. Even these data are not clear. For example, Illinois had pilots in place some time ago; there has been no state-supported program for years, but there were plans for pilots in fall 1999. In Alabama, Maryland, Minnesota, North Dakota, Tennessee, Texas, Virginia, and Wisconsin, pilot programs were started with the intention of expansion at a later date, but these programs never received the expected funding and have operated as pilots for several years now. In these cases, the program pilots remain their only state-supported programs.

CONSIDERATION OR PLANNING UNDER WAY

Seven states—Arkansas, Illinois, Michigan, Missouri, Texas, Vermont, and Wyoming—are currently considering or planning teacher-induction programs or considering statewide funding for these programs. In several of these states, this consideration marks the second or third attempt to establish state-mandated and supported teacher-induction programs. For example, the Illinois state legislature has created a three-tiered certification system with an initial four-year window before standard certification, but requirements for that initial period are not defined. The Illinois State Board of Education has adopted a professional-development framework as state policy and is currently developing drafts of rules and regulations to implement the framework and define an induction period and mentoring support. In this case, tying mentoring support to the state's certification reform initiative likely could result in state funding for a statewide teacher-induction program.

INCORPORATING TEACHING STANDARDS

In addition to state induction programs, a major state-level effort has been under way in recent years to define standards for student learning. Many states are moving toward linking new teacher certification with teaching standards to support better teaching and accountability. In our survey, 14 states reported adopting state standards for teaching: Arkansas, California, Colorado, Connecticut, Indiana, Kentucky, Louisiana, Massachusetts, New Mexico, North Carolina, Oklahoma, Rhode Island, South Carolina, and Tennessee. Seven other states are in the process of considering, defining, or adopting state teaching standards, including Georgia, Illinois, Minnesota, New York, Texas, Wisconsin, and Wyoming. Delaware and Washington, D.C., have a link or plan to develop a link between teacher induction and implementation of student academic standards.

A second variation of the teaching-standards movement is to establish standards specifically designed for new teachers. States taking this approach often use the Interstate New Teacher Assessment and Support Consortium (1991) Standards for Beginning Teachers as the basis for their work. Though several other states are in the process of making this move, Arkansas, California, Connecticut, Illinois, Indiana, Kentucky, Massachusetts, North Carolina, Rhode Island, South Carolina, and Washington, D.C., have completed the work.

A third variation of the teaching-standards movement is to link provision of an initial teaching license or certificate to providing support for new teachers and implementing teaching standards. Supporters argue that new teachers will have a fixed period of time (often 3–4 years) to demonstrate that they have met the standards for "what teachers should know and be able to do"—and that novice teachers deserve the support of a mentor and an induction program to increase their opportunity for success. Issues involved in relating teaching standards to teacher-induction programs will be explored in a later section of this chapter.

OTHER COMMON VARIATIONS FOR STATE PROGRAMS AND SUPPORT

In states with no mandated or state-supported mentoring program, the following variations exist:

- Voluntary programs may or may not be expected to work under the guidance of state policies. In a few cases, the voluntary programs are sponsored by state grants or staff-development funds—or they may be supported by the state teachers' association or a consortium of school districts, universities, or regional service centers. Some have become, by default, statewide induction programs, as in Arizona, Hawaii, Idaho, and Iowa.
- Mentoring is mandated, but mentor programs either are not required, not funded, or not defined by the state. Missouri, Pennsylvania, and Texas are examples of this approach. In Texas, mentors must be assigned, but no program support is provided.
- Other states have no current mandate for a formal teacher-induction program but do provide some non-specific staff-development grants or Goals 2000 mentoring grants to support some level of district induction programs. For example, Oregon's Beginning Teacher Support Program, begun in 1987, collected considerable evidence of its value for both new teachers and mentors. Nevertheless, Oregon lost state funding for its program, due to shortfalls, in 1993. Oregon continues to provide support ($580,000 in 1998) to some 10 district-mentoring programs through its Goals 2000 program. Oregon also continues to make the state mentoring-leadership person available both to guide state work and to support district programs. Several other states provide Goals 2000 and/or staff-development grants to support teacher induction. They include Illinois, Maine, Maryland, Massachusetts, New Hampshire, and South Carolina. Arizona and Utah provide "career ladder" fund-

ing that can support the mentoring role if the local district so chooses.

In some cases, the changes in state induction programs are due to political pressure to improve troublesome aspects of existing programs, such as Florida in 1989, Georgia in 1990, and Louisiana and Virginia in 1991. In other cases, program changes are due to the state's financial condition or priorities. New York's Mentor Teacher/Internship Program, begun in 1986, was funded at increasing levels, reaching $16.5 million until 1991, when all funding was cut. Then, during 1997–98, $10 million in mentor-program support was provided, but no funding was expected for the 1998–99 school year. Such shifts in state policy and support severely impact district planning and programs as well as the quality of mentoring provided to novice teachers. Other state programs that have been cut, or have not been implemented due to lack of state funding, include Alabama, the District of Columbia (1997), Hawaii (1995), Idaho (1992), Illinois (1991), Kansas (1989), Maine, Mississippi (1994), Montana (1995), Nevada (1986), New Mexico, New York (1997), South Dakota (1989), and Tennessee.

In some states, funding and attention to teacher induction has been invested in related initiatives. For example, Kansas rescinded its Kansas Internship Program (1989) after two years of limited funding but has since supported a statewide "results-oriented staff development" initiative. Similarly, Illinois eliminated its mentor-program pilot funding in 1991, about the same time that an extensive, statewide school improvement mandate was funded. In Hawaii (1995), support funds and decisions about teacher-induction programs were moved from state to district level. It is important to note that all of these numbers are in constant flux, as states take periodic steps to develop, rescind, or refine their approaches to programs for novice teachers.

STATE PROGRAMS AS THE CONTEXT FOR LOCAL PROGRAMS

Though this book focuses on preservice and district mentoring programs, local programs exist within a larger context. Whether or not a state has a mandated teacher-induction program and sufficient funding is vitally significant to teacher-induction programs at, at least, the local level. In many cases, state support for local programs influences whether a local program flourishes, merely survives, becomes extinct, or never develops at all.

Also, if a state has a program in place, its approach influences local educators' work with novice teachers. For example, if the state emphasizes novice-teacher assessment by mentors, but the local district prefers that mentors only provide assistance and professional development for novice teachers, a conflict in purpose may surface.

To establish an effective mentoring program, each local district must identify the program purposes, novice teachers' needs, students' needs, and expected results. The district also must develop or refine the program to incorporate best practices in accomplishing those purposes, while responding to state program requirements. The local program in our example must address the state's mandated assessment purpose, but organizers can explore with the state whether the mandate specifically calls for mentors to assess novice teachers or allows novice-teacher assessment in some other way. For the local program to attain its own purpose, organizers must separate mentors from the evaluation process. In essence, the local district is deciding to exceed the state's requirements by incorporating best practices into its local program that are not part of the state program.

In situations like this, the Mentoring Framework can act as a lens to view a state teacher-induction program and can help local program personnel assess the usefulness of their state program as a guide for local programming and practice. Such an assessment may help local program developers determine which dimensions and components of the state program reflect best practice and, therefore, can be used as a guide, and which components may need to be enhanced in the local program.

CONCLUSIONS

Reaching a conclusion about the level of state-mandated and state-supported teacher-induction programs in the United States is difficult. The picture formed is based on data and processes that change from day to day. Still, this survey leads to several broad conclusions about state teacher-induction programs.

- Teacher-induction programs may or may not be mandated or supported at any one time in a particular state, but novice-teacher needs for support, challenge, and guidance are so obvious and well documented that the issue continues to resurface and demand attention, regardless of the state's interest in supporting it. Program solutions based on best practice result in a long-term commitment to teacher induction and a pattern of gradual development and improvement. Solutions that are more political than educational result in varied program support and fragmentary improvement. State departments of education and other educational stakeholder groups must learn from and apply the lessons of these trends.

- Many early state efforts emphasized novice-teacher assessment for certification based primarily on a list of effective teaching practices. Often, these programs concluded that their approaches were too prescriptive or simplistic to define teaching excellence adequately, given the complexity of classrooms and school cultures.

- When state funding has been cut or state programs rescinded, the experience of the program leadership is often lost, or at least unused, as a resource for upcoming decisions about state mandates and programs or for ongoing local programs.

- Federal Goals 2000 funding has allowed several states to maintain support for local district teacher-induction programs, especially in less-populated states and areas where progressive university-based teacher education programs have pursued partnerships with schools.

- The approach of providing assistance through mentoring has varied considerably, from a short-term focus on developing specific teaching practices to a more long-term investment in developing the skills and dispositions for teacher reflection, self-assessment, openness to others' perspectives and feedback, continuous inquiry, and professional growth. The short-term view often is motivated by organizational needs, whereas the long-term view is motivated more by professional needs.

- The state-level processes of defining teaching and student learning standards must be linked to a parallel process of defining standards for effective teacher-induction programs and mentoring practices. That link will increase the probability that mentoring of new teachers will also support the dual agendas of improving teaching and student learning. The Mentoring Framework can guide that linking effort.

- Often, some connections are overlooked between effective teaching and assessment of student learning, effective mentoring of novice teachers as adult learners, and effective novice-teacher mentoring programs. Learning how to become more effective is a multilayered process of interacting initiatives, which can have a multiplying effect if well integrated. Mentors, mentoring-program leaders, and novice teachers must explore the connections between adult and student learning to have an impact beyond helping novice teachers to actual improvement of student learning. For example, just as excellent teaching is based on a cycle of reflection, self-assessment, and refinement of practice (Steffy, Wolfe, Pasch, and Enz 1999), excellent mentors, mentor programs, and their students can benefit from using this same reflective cycle.

The information and documentation assembled during this study of state programs is available on the World Wide Web at: http://www.teachermentors.com/MCenter%20Site/StateList.html. *The words in this chapter are fixed in time, but those on the Web site are not. If you know of inaccuracies, recent changes, or other relevant information concerning any state-level novice-teacher program, please contact Barry Sweeny at 26 W. 413 Grand Ave., Wheaton, IL 60187.*

REFERENCES

American Federation of Teachers. 1998. Mentor teacher programs in the state (Educational Issues Policy Brief #5). Washington, D.C.: AFT.

Barger, R. N. 1986. Survey of Illinois school districts for the initial year of teaching study. Final report. Charleston: Eastern Illinois University. ERIC ED 369 767.

Consortium for Policy Research in Education. 1996. State-mandated and funded new teacher formal induction or mentoring. Philadelphia: University of Pennsylvania.

Defino, M. E., and J. V. Hoffman. 1984. A status report and content analysis of state mandated teacher induction programs. Austin: University of Texas Research and Development Center for Teacher Education. ERIC ED 251 438.

Elias, P., F. J. McDonald, C. Stevenson, R. Simon, and M. L. Fisher. 1980. Study of induction programs for beginning teachers. Volume II. The problems of beginning teachers: A digest of helping programs. Princeton, N.J.: Educational Testing Service. ERIC ED 257 779.

Elias, P., F. J. McDonald, and R. Simon. 1980. Study of induction programs for beginning teachers. Volume III. Helping beginning teachers through the first year: A review of the literature. Princeton, N.J.: Educational Testing Service. ERIC ED 257 780.

Fideler, E. F., and D. Haselkorn, 1999. Learning the ropes: Urban teacher induction programs and practices in the United States. Boston: Recruiting New Teachers.

Furtwengler, C. B. 1993. The reform movement: A fifty-state survey of state actions for beginning teacher programs. Paper presented at the Annual Meeting of the American

Educational Research Association, Atlanta, 12–16 April.

Hawk, P. O., and S. Robards. 1987. Statewide teacher induction programs. In *Teacher induction: A new beginning*, ed. D. M. Brooks, 33–43. Reston, Va.: Association of Teacher Educators.

Hoffman, J., S. Edwards, M. Paulissen, S. O'Neal, and S. A. Barnes. 1985. A study of state-mandated beginning teacher programs and their effects. *Journal of Teacher Education* 37(1): 16–21.

Interstate New Teacher Assessment and Support Consortium. 1991. *Model standards for beginning teacher licensing and development: A resource for state dialogue.* Washington, D.C.: Council of Chief State School Officers.

McDonald, F. J. 1980a. Study of induction programs for beginning teachers. Executive summary. Princeton, N.J.: Educational Testing Service. ERIC ED 257 776.

McDonald, F. J. 1980b. Study of induction programs for beginning teachers. Volume I. The problems of beginning teachers: A crisis in training. Princeton, N.J.: Educational Testing Service. ERIC ED 257 778.

Neuweiler, H. B., comp. 1988. Teacher education policy in the states: A fifty-state survey of legislative and administrative actions. Washington D.C.: American Association of Colleges for Teacher Education. ERIC ED 296 997.

Sclan, E., and L. Darling-Hammond. 1992. Beginning teacher performance evaluation: An overview of state policies. Washington, D.C.: ERIC Clearinghouse on Teacher Education. ERIC ED 341 689.

Simon, R., comp. 1980. Study of induction programs for beginning teachers. Volume IV. Educators interested and involved in programs for beginning teachers: A human resource bank. Princeton, N.J.: Educational Testing Service. ERIC ED 257 781.

Steffy, B. E., M. P. Wolfe, S. H. Pasch, and B. J. Enz, eds. 1999. *Life cycle of the career teacher.* Thousand Oaks, Calif.: Corwin.

Sweeny, B. W. 1998. What's happening in mentoring & induction in each of the United States? Wheaton, Ill.: Resources for Staff & Organization Development. Available at: *http://www.teachermentors.com/MCenter%20Site/StateList.html.*

11

Rich Sources—An Annotated Mentoring Bibliography

by Carol A. Bartell, Barbara D. Day, Fay A. Head, and Alan J. Reiman

The rich sources in this selected annotated mentoring bibliography are provided for those who would like additional information. This bibliography is not designed to be exhaustive. We have included seminal works on mentoring as well as a representative sample of the research on mentoring during the period 1985–99. To make this annotated bibliography as "user friendly" as possible, we have divided it into seven sections:

- Texts, Collections, Reviews of the Literature, and Annotated Bibliographies;
- Individual Studies Related to the Mentoring Framework;
- Journal Theme Issues on Mentoring;
- Monographs Produced by Professional Organizations;
- ERIC Documents Related to the Mentoring Framework;
- Dissertations Related to the Mentoring Framework; and
- Literature from Other Academic Disciplines Related to the Mentoring Framework.

TEXTS, COLLECTIONS, REVIEWS OF THE LITERATURE, AND ANNOTATED BIBLIOGRAPHIES

Beasley, K., D. Corbin, S. Feiman-Nemser, and C. Shank. 1997. Making it happen: Creating a sub-culture of mentoring in a professional development school. In *Making professional development schools work: Politics, practice and policy,* ed. M. Levine and R. Trachtman, 33–51. New York: Teachers College Press.

Drawing on journals written during a three-year period, this chapter describes a unique peer-mentoring project implemented by three teachers and a teacher educator in a professional-development school. The chapter shows how mentoring, professional development, teacher learning, and teacher research came together as two teachers helped their colleague, a veteran of 22 years, create a learner-centered classroom and transform her teaching practice.

DeBolt, G. P., ed. 1992. *Teacher induction and mentoring: School-based collaborative programs.* Albany: State University of New York Press.

This book provides an overview of the induction into teaching and mentoring processes, describes five effective school-based models, and reports the results of a large-scale study of the most helpful elements identified by experienced mentor teachers.

Feiman-Nemser, S. 1998. Teachers as teacher educators. *European Journal of Teacher Education* 21(1): 63–74.

Why don't teachers in mentor-type roles always see themselves as teacher educators? How can teachers become thoughtful teachers of teaching? What does "educative" mentoring mean, and what does it entail? Drawing on firsthand experience and findings from a comparative, cross-cultural study of mentored learning to teach, the author explores these questions.

Feiman-Nemser, S., and K. Beasley. 1997. Mentoring as assisted performance: The case of co-planning. In *Constructivist teacher education: Building a world of new understanding,* ed. V. Richardson, 108–26. Washington, D.C.: Falmer.

This chapter examines one extended mentoring episode—a two-hour session in which a mentor and a novice co-plan a language arts unit around the works of Leonard Everett Fisher, an award-winning children's author/illustrator. Drawing on sociocultural theories of learning, the authors use this case to develop a conception of mentoring as joint participation in authentic activity. This conception differs from conventional views of mentoring as providing emotional support or practical advice.

Feiman-Nemser, S., M. Parker, and K. Zeichner. 1993. Are mentor teachers teacher educators? In *Mentoring: Perspectives on school-based practice,* ed. D. McIntyre, H. Hagger, and M. Wilkin, 147–65. London, England: Kogan Page.

This chapter draws on a study of mentoring in an alternate-route program in a large urban school district. In this program, teacher trainees teach full-time in junior and senior high schools while participating in a two-year, district-sponsored training program leading to a teaching credential. The authors analyze the content of mentor training and present three illustrative cases of mentor/trainee interactions. They argue that mentors focus on performance rather than the ideas behind the performance and do not help trainees connect their actions to student learning.

Fideler, E. F., and D. Haselkorn. 1999. *Learning the ropes: Urban teacher induction programs and practices in the United States.* Boston: Recruiting New Teachers.

This book provides an extensive overview of teacher-induction programs in urban contexts across the country. The recent history of teacher induction is provided, describing ways that mentoring is key to educational practice. A survey of teacher-induction programs across all the states is complemented by an in-depth study of ten of the urban programs. Recommendations are also offered for subsequent study and practice.

Galvez-Hjornevik, C. 1986. Mentoring among teachers: A review of the literature. *Journal of Teacher Education* 37(1): 190–94.

This literature review is a "classic" that provides an excellent overview of mentoring literature through 1986.

Gold, Y. 1996. Beginning teacher support: Attrition, mentoring, and induction. In *Handbook of research on teacher education: A project of the Association of Teacher Educators*, 2d ed., ed. J. Sikula, T. Buttery, and E. Guyton, 548–94. New York: Macmillan.

This review of the literature considers the rationale and impetus for beginning-teacher support, the nature and elements of effective support, and types of support and induction programs already under way. Mentoring is examined as a central feature of induction programs. The author raises critical issues and persistent concerns, presenting emerging conceptions and promising practices. An extensive reference list is provided.

Hawkey, K. 1997. Roles, responsibilities, and relationships in mentoring: A literature review and agenda for research. *Journal of Teacher Education* 48(5): 325–35.

This article reviews literature on the nature of interactions between student teachers and mentors, examining approaches to research into mentoring (roles and responsibilities of participants, stages in student teacher development, stages in mentoring relationships, and personal perspectives, values, and assumptions). Dynamics in mentoring relationships are discussed, as well as the need for further research on mentoring relationships.

Huling-Austin, L. 1990. Teacher induction programs and internships. In *Handbook of research on teacher education: A project of the Association of Teacher Educators,* ed. W. R. Houston, M. Haberman, and J. Sikula, 535–48. New York: Macmillan.

This review of the literature provides the background and history of teacher induction and addresses policy developments as well as conceptual paradigms for teacher-induction programs. In addition, research studies that have influenced the goals of teacher induction are identified. Points of consensus and controversy regarding teacher induction are reviewed, and next steps are suggested for future research.

Huling-Austin, L. 1992. Research on learning to teach: Implications for teacher induction and mentoring programs. *Journal of Teacher Education* 43(3): 173–80.

More than 80 studies of learning to teach are reviewed for implications for induction and mentoring programs. The author summarizes issues that must be addressed, including reduced teaching loads for beginning teachers, multiple opportunities to teach the same content, support from peers and experienced colleagues, and formative evaluation that differs from the summative evaluation of experienced teachers.

Huling-Austin, L., S. J. Odell, P. Ishler, R. S. Kay, and R. A. Edelfelt, eds. 1989. *Assisting the beginning teacher.* Reston, Va.: Association of Teacher Educators.

The purpose of this book is to help practitioners and policy makers understand how important it is to assist beginning teachers, and what it involves in terms of policy, procedures, pitfalls, personnel, cost in time and money, and prospects. Chapters include: "Beginning Teacher Assistance Programs: An Overview"; "Developing Support Programs for Beginning Teachers"; "Research on Beginning Teacher Assistance Programs"; "Impact of Beginning Teacher Assistance Programs"; "Evaluation of Beginning Teacher Assistance Programs"; and "Starting a Beginning Teacher Assistance Program."

Little, J. W. 1990. The mentor phenomenon and the social organization of teaching. In *Review of research in education,* ed. C. B. Cazden, 297–351. Washington, D.C.: American Educational Research Association.

This chapter provides an extensive review of mentoring as it relates to the social organization of teaching. The author offers insightful observations of the current state of teacher mentoring. The etiology of mentoring is provided, including a critical analysis of formal mentor roles, the conservative precedent of teaching contexts, the problems with identifying expertise in teaching for mentors, and the problem of mentors being considered experts among other teachers. Mentoring in teacher-induction contexts is discussed.

Odell, S. J. 1990. *Mentor teacher programs: What the research says to the teacher.* Washington, D.C.: National Education Association.

> This monograph surveys the literature and provides a broad understanding of the concept of mentoring and its application to teaching. A synthesis of research on mentoring is presented, including an explication of the origin, value, and essence of the mentoring concept; the rationale for mentoring beginning teachers; and mentoring goals. The author envisions a four-phase mentoring process: (1) developing the relationship, preferably outside the teaching day; (2) mutually determining the mentoring content; (3) applying effective mentoring styles and strategies, generally relating to initiator- or responder-type styles and directive or non-directive strategies; and (4) disengaging the relationship so that the beginning teacher will not feel trauma but will be able to organize colleague-support networks.

Reiman, A. J., and L. Thies-Sprinthall. 1998. *Mentoring and supervision for teacher development.* New York: Longman.

> This book summarizes the current literature related to teacher supervision and mentoring practices. It synthesizes the fields of instructional supervision, adult development, teacher education and mentoring, and ongoing professional development. Supervision, as used in this text, refers to a school-based or school/college-based activity that improves instruction through guided assistance and discourse between adults.

Stewart, D. K. 1992. Mentoring in beginning teacher induction: Studies in the ERIC database. *Journal of Teacher Education* 43(3): 222–26.

> This article lists studies in the ERIC database related to mentoring. The bibliography is limited to journal articles and documents entered into the database since 1990. Citations focus on articles and documents dealing with analysis of mentoring and induction programs.

Veenman, S. 1984. Perceived problems of beginning teachers. *Review of Educational Research* 54(2): 143–78.

> Studies from different countries on perceived problems of beginning teachers are reviewed. Issues discussed include reality shock; behavior and attitude change; situational and individual differences; principals' views; job satisfaction; teacher education; and in-service support. Three frameworks of teacher development provide conceptualizations of individual differences among beginning teachers.

Zimpher, N. L., and S. R. Rieger. 1988. Mentoring teachers: What are the issues? *Theory into Practice* 27(3): 175–82.

> This review of literature related to the issues associated with teacher mentoring explores various ways to construe mentor roles, formal and

informal mentoring processes, supportive conditions for mentoring, criteria for selecting mentors, and criteria for matching mentors to beginning teachers. A strong case is made for preparation and support of mentor teachers.

INDIVIDUAL STUDIES RELATED TO THE MENTORING FRAMEWORK (1985–99)

Abell, S. K., D. R. Dillon, C. J. Hopkins, W. D. McInerney, and D. G. O'Brien. 1995. 'Somebody to count on': Mentor/intern relationships in a beginning teacher internship program. *Teaching and Teacher Education* 11(2): 173–88.

Mentor and intern relationships in a beginning-teacher internship program are examined. Interviews with mentors and interns indicate that they jointly constructed their relationships, which were undergirded by mutual respect and trust.

Barnard, N. 1988. Tough love for the new boys and girls (United Kingdom government plans induction year for new teachers). *Times Educational Supplement* (London), 8 May, A21(1).

The British government planned to introduce a new form of induction year for new teachers in September 1999. Under the planned regulations, new teachers will teach only 90 percent of the average contact time for other teachers in their school. Their career-entry profile will contain targets and an action plan for their first year. There will also be a general program of training and support for new teachers. It will be necessary for new teachers to meet national standards set by the Teacher Training Agency for Qualified Teacher Status.

Bartell, C. A. 1995. Shaping teacher induction policy in California. *Teacher Education Quarterly* 22(4): 27–43.

The California New Teacher Project was established to pilot support and assessment strategies designed to: retain capable teachers; improve the teaching abilities of beginning teachers; improve the teaching of students of diverse backgrounds; and identify beginning teachers who need additional assistance or must be advised to go into other professions. The four-year pilot demonstrated that well-planned programs of sufficient intensity had the most likelihood of achieving the intended outcomes. Essential features included: trained, experienced teachers serving as mentors; scheduled time for teachers to work together; professional development appropriate to new-teacher needs and levels of development; and assessment and feedback of teaching development.

Bullough, R. V., Jr. 1990. Supervision, mentoring, and self-discovery: A case study of a first-year teacher. *Journal of Curriculum and Supervision* 5(4): 338–60.

This case traces a teacher's changing metaphors of teaching and the relationship between supervisor and teacher throughout the initial year. The beginner establishes a tentative, cautious relationship with the supervisor or mentor that discourages openness. The researcher indicates that finding oneself as a teacher and establishing a professional identity are conspicuously missing from most lists of beginning teachers' problems.

Carter, K. 1988. Using cases to frame mentor-novice conversations about teaching. *Theory into Practice* 27(3): 214–22.

The use of case literature by mentor teachers to convey theoretical knowledge to beginning teachers and to promote reflection and analysis is explored. The article addresses the advantages for mentors, beginning teachers, and the school. Possible topics are suggested, and potential obstacles are noted.

Christensen, J. E., and D. F. Conway. 1991. The use of self-selected mentors by beginning and new-to-district teachers. *Action in Teacher Education* 12(4): 21–28.

A questionnaire survey of beginning and new-to-district teachers in a large school district studied use of self-selected mentors. Teachers indicated they did self-select mentors generally from the same area or grade level. Most needed mentors to provide information on policy and procedures. All perceived the experience as valuable.

Cochran-Smith, M. 1991. Learning to teach against the grain. *Harvard Educational Review* 61(3): 279–310.

This study examines the conversations of student teachers and experienced teachers in weekly, school-site meetings at four urban schools. These occasions for group mentoring exposed novices to broad themes of reform through discussions of highly contextualized problems of practice.

Danielson, C. 1996. *Enhancing professional practice: A framework for teaching*. Alexandria, Va.: Association for Supervision and Curriculum Development.

Educational Testing Service's PRAXIS III assessment criteria are used to identify those aspects of a teacher's abilities that promote student learning. The author extrapolates what teachers should know and be able to do in their profession in the categories of: planning and preparation; classroom environment; instruction; and professional responsibilities. This framework is designed to address the concerns of novice teachers and to help experienced mentor teachers improve their colleagues' effectiveness.

Feigen, S. M., and R. A. Sandlin. 1995. Collaboration between the university and school district: Can it work? *Teacher Education Quarterly* 22(4): 75–82.

This article investigates the features of well-managed, collaborative induction programs between universities and school districts. Features include: consistent leadership and administration; sufficient time allocated for project directors to administer local projects; players' positions that were sufficiently influential in both; project directors familiar with local organizational contexts; one agency designated as lead; and clear division of responsibilities and delegation of duties.

Feiman-Nemser, S., and M. B. Parker. 1990. Making subject matter part of the conversation in learning to teach. *Journal of Teacher Education* 41(3): 32–43.

Conversations between four mentor and four novice teachers are analyzed to discover how they discuss issues about teaching and learning of content. Analysis of conversations reveals several ways that mentors deal with novices' understanding of subject matter. Conversations are discussed using four aspects of learning to teach content.

Feiman-Nemser, S., and M. B. Parker. 1992. *Mentoring in context: A comparison of two U.S. programs for beginning teachers.* East Lansing, Mich.: National Center for Research on Teacher Learning.

This study describes how the contexts of mentoring shape the perspectives and practices of mentors in two innovative programs. The Teacher Trainee Program in Los Angeles is an effort to recruit teacher candidates for inner-city secondary schools by providing on-the-job training to college graduates. The Graduate Intern Program in Albuquerque extends preservice preparation by offering structured support to beginning elementary teachers. Three perspectives on mentoring are identified in relation to teacher induction: (1) casting mentors as local guides; (2) casting mentors as educational companions; and (3) viewing mentors as agents of cultural change.

Feiman-Nemser, S., and M. B. Parker. 1993. Mentoring in context: A comparison of two U.S. programs for beginning teachers. *International Journal of Educational Research* 19(8): 699–718.

This study compares two beginning-teacher programs. Researchers document striking differences in the way mentor teachers conceive of and execute their work with novices. They link these differences in mentors' perspectives and practices to differences in role expectations, working conditions, program orientations, and mentor preparation.

Fielding, M. 1999a. An eye on the experts (First appointments: Newly qualified teachers should seek advice from experienced colleagues). *Times*

Educational Supplement (London), 8 January, D14(2).

Newly qualified teachers should obtain advice from more experienced colleagues, even though they may feel nervous about asking for help. They should turn to experienced colleagues who are still enthusiastic about teaching rather than those who reject and challenge change. When seeking advice, it is important to be specific about concerns. Novices should listen to advice carefully, but not necessarily follow it without considering its appropriateness.

Fielding, M. 1999b. Here's looking at you (First appointments: Newly qualified teachers can benefit from having lessons observed). *Times Educational Supplement* (London), 8 January, D15(1).

Newly qualified teachers must accept that having their lessons observed is a valuable way to develop their skills, even if they do not like this process. Observing lessons must have a clear purpose and focus on just one element of the teacher's performance. There should be detailed feedback as soon as possible following the observation. In many cases, the presence of additional adults creates a more civilized atmosphere in the classroom.

Franke, A., and L. O. Dahlgren. 1996. Conceptions of mentoring: An empirical study of conceptions of mentoring during the school-based teacher education. *Teaching and Teacher Education* 12(6): 627–41.

To determine conceptions of mentoring, Swedish researchers videotaped mentoring sessions between student teachers and their cooperating teachers and conducted interviews with both groups. Data analysis indicates that the two groups had different conceptions about the function of mentoring and its content and form.

Ganser, T. 1995. What are the concerns and questions of mentors of beginning teachers? *NASSP Bulletin* 79(575): 83–91.

A survey of 92 mentor teachers resulted in 210 comments. About half focused on the mentoring role, and half related to perceived obstacles to effective mentoring. Respondents often doubted their mentoring qualifications and voiced concerns about time, pairing methods, beginning teachers' receptiveness, and limited support for mentoring activities.

Ganser, T. 1996. Preparing mentors of beginning teachers: An overview for staff developers. *Journal of Staff Development* 17(4): 8–11.

Focusing on the benefits of mentoring for beginning teachers, this article reviews common goals and organizational formats for mentoring programs, outlines basic knowledge and skills necessary for effective mentoring, suggests resources useful in preparing teachers to serve as mentors, and examines issues about mentoring for staff developers.

Ganser, T. 1998. Metaphors for mentoring. *The Educational Forum* 62(2): 113–19.

In a survey of 124 teachers who mentored beginning teachers, 98 described mentoring in terms of metaphors related to interpersonal relationships, teaching, problem prevention, direction, and growth/creativity. Metaphors revealed a wide range of mentoring approaches, and discussion of them was thought useful to mentors and their protégés.

Garten, T. R., J. A. Hudson, and H. A. Gossen. 1993. Teacher induction using a shared lesson design model. *NASSP Bulletin* 77(554): 76–81.

This study examines the relationship between university instruction and classroom performance by new teachers using a commonly accepted eight-element lesson design within a teacher-preparation program. The survey provided clear evidence that the supervising teachers had received preparation and were able to implement the lesson-design model successfully. Interestingly, of the eight elements included in the lesson design, closure was recognized as being used least effectively.

Garten, T. R., J. A. Hudson, and H. A. Gossen. 1994. Preparing mentors of first-year teachers: Practitioner/professor collaborative experience. *Teaching Education* 6(1): 123–32.

First-year teachers need mentoring by experienced, successful practitioners. This paper suggests a model for preparing mentors developed by school district personnel and university faculty. The model provides 14 hours (distributed over the school year) of training in philosophy, basic mentoring, communication skills, peer supervision, observation skills, and conferencing.

Gay, G. 1995. Modeling and mentoring in urban teacher preparation. *Education and Urban Society* 28(1): 103–18.

This article offers suggestions for using modeling and mentoring in urban teacher education in the belief that the power of models and mentors resides more in their being and behaving than in the finished products. Good role models live their ethics and beliefs personally and professionally.

Gehrke, N. J. 1988a. Toward a definition of mentoring. *Theory into Practice* 27(3): 190–94.

A "classic" in the mentoring literature that has helped form a conceptual foundation for the mentoring of teachers. An attempt to define teacher mentorship begins with a personal account of experiences as both a protégé and a mentor, leading to a discussion of mentoring as a "gift-exchange" process, with mentors helping others to develop different perspectives and protégés passing this gift of reflection to others.

Gehrke, N. J. 1988b. On preserving the essence of mentoring as one form of teacher leadership. *Journal of Teacher Education* 31(1): 43–45.

The mentor-protégé relationship contains many elements of other important human relationships. In particular, mentoring is described within the framework of Martin Buber's "I-Thou" theory. Steps to encourage such relationships are given.

Gersten, R., J. Woodward, and M. Morvant. 1992. Refining the working knowledge of experienced teachers. *Educational Leadership* 49(7): 34–38.

An emerging view of professional development recommends enhancement of current practice by integrating research-based strategies into teachers' classroom repertoires. This article describes an urban elementary school enhancement program involving intensive collaboration between teachers and master teachers. Two case studies are described.

Giebelhaus, C., and M. Bendixon-Noe. 1997. Mentoring: Help or hindrance? *Midwestern Researcher* 10(4): 20–23.

The paper discusses many of the problems inherent in mentoring programs. Mentoring programs historically lack definition, mentor training, and selection of effective mentors. This lack of clarity often overshadows the potential advantages of mentoring programs. This critical examination may help to pinpoint selection, training, and matching criteria for improving mentor programs.

Gold, K. 1999. It's never too soon to care (First appointments: Pastoral skills for newly qualified teachers). *Times Educational Supplement* (London), 8 January, D20(2).

Newly qualified teachers ideally should not have to take responsibility for a tutor group, but this does not mean that they will avoid all pastoral tasks. For this reason, they should try to gain a clear insight into the accepted ways of seeking help and guidance for pupils with social difficulties. It will not be possible for newly qualified teachers to devote time to counseling courses, but they should attempt to obtain ideas from colleagues and department heads.

Goodman, J. 1987. Factors in becoming a proactive elementary school teacher: A preliminary study of selected novices. *Journal of Education for Teaching* 13(3): 207–29.

Proactive teachers are defined as those likely to be thoughtful, experimental, responsible, and autonomous. Factors in their development include: their own personal knowledge base, talent, and commitment to become reflective decision makers; the institutional support they received as novice teachers; the time they had to pursue activities that reflected their goals; and the response to their efforts from their pupils.

Graham, P. 1997. Tensions in the mentor teacher-student teacher relationship: Creating productive sites for learning within a high school English teacher education program. *Teaching and Teacher Education* 13(5): 513–27.

This study focuses on two divisive patterns of tension within mentor relationships with student teachers. Philosophical differences and tolerance for uncertainty are examined within a teacher education program for high school English based on collaborative inquiry and teacher research. Interviews, observations, and written documents highlight five differences in principles and processes that support more effective ways to handle tensions.

Gray, W. A., and M. M. Gray. 1985. Synthesis of research on mentoring beginning teachers. *Educational Leadership* 43(3): 37–43.

This paper reviews research on mentors and covers mentor characteristics, behaviors, and roles. In addition, matching mentors and protégés and the needs of beginning teachers are addressed. The authors also discuss changes in the mentor-protégé relationship that occur as protégés gain experience and need mentors less.

Guyton, E., and F. Hidalgo. 1995. Characteristics, responsibilities, and qualities of urban school mentors. *Education and Urban Society* 28(1): 40–47.

This paper describes how teacher mentors in urban schools need particular characteristics to promote development in beginning teachers because of the urban school's unique environment. Urban mentor teachers must be able to articulate their beliefs and practices and have well-developed coaching skills.

Head, F. A. 1992. Student teaching as initiation into the teaching profession. *Anthropology & Education Quarterly* 23(2): 89–107.

This study examines student teaching as it relates to the liminal (threshold) phase of a rite of passage. The use of mentors is of key importance in rites of passage. Thus, much can be learned regarding the mentoring of preservice student teachers through the lens of an anthropological rite of passage.

Head, F. A., and M. M. Gray. 1988. The legacy of Mentor: Insights into Western history, literature, and the media. *International Journal of Mentoring* 2(2): 26–33.

The concept of mentoring is intimately related to its historical roots in the man Mentor, whose protégé was the son of Ulysses. Other famous mentors such as Fenelon, who not only mentored Louis XIV's son but was also a major literary and historical figure of his time, have had profound impacts upon our Western media, literature, and history.

Head, F. A., A. J. Reiman, and L. Thies-Sprinthall. 1992. The reality of mentoring: Complexity in its process and function. In *Mentoring: Contemporary principles and issues,* ed. T. M. Bey and C. T. Holmes, 5–24. Reston, Va.: Association of Teacher Educators.

As the Mentoring Framework of this volume depicts, true mentoring is quite complex in both its process and functions. This chapter in a prior mentoring monograph explores the complexity of mentoring in depth and offers suggestions for implementation, so that the "heart and soul" of mentoring are not lost when applied as a popular educational innovation.

Hidalgo, F. 1987. The evolving of first-year junior high school teachers in difficult settings: Three case studies. *Action in Teacher Education* 8(4): 75–79.

Three case studies of beginning but not-yet-certified teachers in predominantly Hispanic junior high schools in an urban environment show: how the beginning teachers' concerns evolve; how their concerns compare with beginning teachers in similar environments who are fully credentialed; and how various factors influence teachers' patterns of concern. Cases were drawn from interviews and responses to a stages-of-concern questionnaire administered at the beginning, middle, and end of the school year.

Holmes, E. 1998. Your initiation rights (First appointments: Induction programs for newly qualified teachers). *Times Educational Supplement* (London), 9 January, B10(2).

Newly qualified teachers in the United Kingdom are likely to benefit considerably from the induction year contained in the Teaching and Higher Education Bill (implemented in June 1998) and from the career-entry profile drawn up by the Teacher Training Agency. However, they will still face many challenges once they actually start their first teaching jobs. For this reason, newly qualified teachers should carefully determine if they can expect structured support from their particular schools.

Howey, K. R. 1988. Mentor-teachers as inquiring professionals. *Theory into Practice* 27(3): 209–13.

This article is part of a mentoring theme issue for *Theory into Practice.* The author discusses the importance of mentors viewing themselves and their teaching practices as professionals. Reflection upon all aspects of teaching and mentoring enhances the quality of these roles and improves mentors' satisfaction and efficacy.

Huang, S. L., and H. C. Waxman. 1995. Beginning and mentor teachers' perceptions of their urban school-level work environment. *Spectrum* 13(1): 11–17.

The researchers queried 150 first-year teachers and 150 mentor teachers from 86 Southern urban schools regarding their work environment and professional aspirations. Questionnaires addressed affiliation, professional interest, resource adequacy, and work pressure. Resource adequacy influenced beginning teachers' intentions to continue teaching. Mentor teachers perceived their work environments more favorably than did beginning teachers.

Huffman, G., and S. Leak. 1986. Beginning teachers' perceptions of mentors. *Journal of Teacher Education* 37(1): 22–25.

The purpose of this research is to describe and assess the roles that mentor teachers play in a program for beginning teachers. Participants strongly endorsed the mentor role as important to the induction process. Mentors provide assistance in addressing needs through encouragement, collegiality, and helpful suggestions for improvement of teaching skills. Beginning teachers cited the following as the most helpful roles their mentors played: providing practical assistance and information, sharing ideas and instructional materials, suggesting strategies for organization of time and classroom management, and providing feedback and evaluation. The most common concern was the need for more informal conferencing time between mentor and beginning teacher.

Hyink, B. G., and F. A. Head. 1990. You scratch my back; I'll scratch yours: University/public school research collaboration. *Phi Delta Kappan* 72(4): 327–28.

Effective collaboration among all constituents in a mentoring program is essential. This study discusses a highly effective collaborative effort that is a mutual "win-win" for all parties involved. Particularly in a time of diminishing resources for mentoring, creative collaboration that benefits all participants is most important.

Janas, M. 1996. Mentoring the mentor: A challenge for staff development. *Journal of Staff Development* 17(4): 2–5.

Staff development is crucial in creating successful mentoring relationships in schools and districts. Four major tasks for staff developers creating mentoring programs are: selecting and training mentors, matching mentors with protégés, setting goals and expectations, and establishing the program.

Kerrins, J. A. 1995. A teacher-centered induction experience. *Journal of Staff Development* 16(1): 26–30.

A teacher-induction seminar was implemented in a school district in Colorado to promote professional development and to facilitate new teachers' transition into the district. The seminar transcripts reveal that, over a period of time, questions move from routine issues to more pedagogical questions. Seminar participants developed friendships with one another and saw other members as a support system for venting feelings and problem solving.

Kilgore, K., D. Ross, and J. Zbikowski. 1990. Understanding the teaching perspectives of first-year teachers. *Journal of Teacher Education* 41(1): 28–38.

The researchers examine the effect of the school context on the reflective attitudes of six first-year teachers. Factors include: teachers' sense of job satisfaction and success, principals' administrative style, faculty collegiality, teacher autonomy in decision making, and teacher-support systems. They find that teachers exhibited reflective attitudes that were nurtured in a supportive context in which teachers were viewed as professionals, encouraged to explore the complexity of their problems, and given the autonomy to experiment with curriculum and instructional strategies.

Killion, J. P. 1990. The benefits of an induction program for experienced teachers. *Journal of Staff Development* 11(4): 32–36.

The author demonstrates that new teachers are not the only ones to benefit from an induction program. Such a program holds promise for promoting growth, recognition, experience-enhancing roles, and collegiality for mid- to late-career teachers who serve as mentors.

Klausmeier, R. L., Jr. 1994. Responsibilities and strategies of successful mentors. *The Clearing House* 68(1): 27–29.

This article focuses on characteristics of effective mentors. Strategies for mentors, including personal and emotional development, effective instructional strategies, classroom-management techniques, and interactional strategies are described.

Mitchell, D. E., L. D. Scott, and I. G. Hendrick. 1996. *California mentor teacher program evaluation*. Riverside: California Educational Research Cooperative.

State law established the California Mentor Teacher Program in 1983 primarily as an incentive plan for experienced teachers. This study confirms the primary role for mentors as providing assistance and guidance to fellow teachers, especially new teachers. Local programs that experienced the most program integration also reported consistently higher impact on beginning-teacher performance, instruction, curriculum, student performance, teacher morale and status, student assessment, retention of good teachers, and performance evaluations.

Moir, E., and C. Stobbe. 1995. Professional growth for new teachers: Support and assessment through collegial partnerships. *Teacher Education Quarterly* 22(4): 83–91.

The researchers describe the importance of structuring dialogue between advisor and new teacher around issues and problems of practice. They find that structured interactions and commitment toward professional growth between these partners create an atmosphere that encourages new teachers to develop norms and standards for professional collegiality, inquiry, reflection, and assessment. Through these experiences, new teachers enter the profession with the expectations that teaching is collegial; that the profession requires a continuous cycle of teaching, assessment, reflection, and re-teaching; and that learning to teach is a lifelong process.

Morgon, M. 1997. Dear colleague: A letter from a new teacher to experienced teachers (Special section: Teacher Leadership). *The Clearing House* 70(5): 250(3).

A first-year teacher writes to more experienced teachers asking for support in practical information, political savoir faire, and professional concerns. The novice teacher claims that any help extended to him by his experienced colleagues will make him feel like a joint member in the school community.

Nilssen, V., S. Gudmundsdottir, and V. Wangsmo-Cappelen. 1998. Mentoring the teaching of multiplication: A case study. *European Journal of Teacher Education* 21(1): 29–45.

This case study tells the story of Vibeke, a student teacher on her last teaching practice before graduating from her teacher education program, and her interactions with her mentor, who is also her teaching-practice supervisor. Within a few weeks, Vibeke will be considered a fully qualified teacher; thus, she is ready, in theory, to teach any subject in the ten grades compulsory in the Norwegian school system. This study describes Vibeke teaching multiplication to second graders (8-year-old students) in a primary school in Trondheim. The description makes it clear that, though Vibeke is only a few weeks from graduating, she has a great deal to learn about teaching multiplication to second-grade students.

Odell, S. J. 1991/92. Mentoring beginning teachers in restructured elementary schools: A natural link. *SRATE Journal* 1(1): 36–39.

This article addresses structural, personnel, and pedagogical considerations pertaining to the development of beginning-teacher mentoring programs in the context of restructured elementary schools. Research indicates that restructured schools provide a natural environment for fostering successful mentoring experiences because of their empowered teachers, participative decision making, and school-university collaboration.

Odell, S. J., and D. P. Ferraro. 1992. Teacher mentoring and teacher retention. *Journal of Teacher Education* 43(3): 200–204.

This qualitative study traces two cohorts of beginning elementary teachers who had participated for a year in a collaborative university-school system teacher-mentoring program to determine how many were still teaching four years later. Trained mentors provided weekly mentoring support during the first two years of these beginning teachers' careers. After four years, approximately 96 percent of those located were still teaching. These beginning teachers stated they most valued emotional support from their mentors during this program. The study suggests that teacher mentoring may reduce early attrition of beginning teachers.

Perez, K., C. Swain, and C. S. Hartsough. 1997. An analysis of practices used to support new teachers. *Teacher Education Quarterly* 24(12): 41–52.

The researchers find that coaching, mentoring, and seminars are all successful strategies to provide support to new teachers. Practices perceived to be most effective were interactive activities and blending apprenticeships and mentoring.

Raywid, M. A. 1993. Finding time for collaboration. *Educational Leadership* 51(1): 30–34.

Time for teachers to collaborate to undertake and sustain school improvement may be more important than equipment, facilities, or even staff development. Though some schools manage to include pupil-free workdays in their annual calendars, others must find low-cost alternatives. This article presents 15 examples involving creative scheduling or instructional groupings favoring teacher collaboration.

Reiman, A. J., F. A. Head, and L. Thies-Sprinthall. 1992. Collaboration and mentoring. In *Mentoring: Contemporary principles and issues,* ed. T. M. Bey and C. T. Holmes, 79–93. Reston, Va.: Association of Teacher Educators.

Collaboration is a crucial aspect of successful mentoring programs. This chapter, from a prior mentoring monograph, discusses successful collaborative practices in a nationally recognized, exemplary mentoring program.

Rosenholtz, S. J. 1989. Workplace conditions that affect teacher quality and commitment: Implications for teacher induction programs. *The Elementary School Journal* 89(4): 421–39.

This research identifies organizational conditions that contribute to teachers' commitment to schools and outlines how schools can be structured to enhance teachers' learning opportunities and sense of teaching efficacy. The research makes recommendations for the design of teacher-induction programs, suggesting that psychic rewards, increased task autonomy and discretion, and meaningfulness of work play important roles in fostering teacher success. Such workplace conditions help new teachers feel confident about their classroom practices, believe that student learning is possible, and sense that they are making a sufficient difference in the lives of their students.

Schaffer, E. 1992. An innovative beginning teacher induction program: A two-year analysis of classroom interactions. *Journal of Teacher Education* 43(3): 181–92.

This article describes a two-year, collaborative, university-school teacher-induction program in which beginning teachers' classroom performances were assessed using a behavioral observation instrument. Participants made significant gains, with first-year gains resulting from improvements in classroom organization and second-year gains related to changes in more intellectually complex teaching areas.

Shulman, J. H., and J. A. Colbert, eds. 1988. *Mentor teacher casebooks.* San Francisco: Far West Laboratory for Educational Research and Development.

These two volumes of mentor-teacher case studies provide a varied tapestry of mentoring relationships. Insightful questions challenge mentors and teacher educators to consider foundational issues raised in each of the case studies presented.

Stallion, B. K., and N. L. Zimpher. 1991. Classroom management intervention: The effects of training and mentoring on the inductee teacher's behavior. *Action in Teacher Education* 13(1): 42–50.

This study assesses a classroom-management program embedded in an induction program for mentors and beginning teachers. Researchers assigned mentor-beginning teacher pairs to treatment conditions. Some pairs completed a midyear classroom-management intervention workshop. Trained teachers received higher ratings than untrained ones. The presence of mentors did not make significant differences in results for this study.

Stark, S. 1991. Toward an understanding of the beginning-teacher experience: Curricular insights for teacher education. *Journal of Curriculum and Supervision* 6(4): 294–311.

This article studies how teaching is influenced by prior beliefs and experiences but develops in a specific context. The research reveals and interprets the meanings of two teachers' first-year teaching experiences. Through dialogue and written reflections, meaning and understanding unfolded, and significant themes emerged for each participant.

Stevens, N. H. 1995. R and R for mentors: Renewal and reaffirmation for mentors as benefits from the mentoring experience. *Educational Horizons* 73(3): 130–37.

This researcher investigated the ways mentors perceive that their own attitudes and classroom performance change due to the mentoring experience. Mentors in Philadelphia were found to grow professionally as a result of their participation. Mentoring was found to promote the professionalism of teachers. Mentors tended to be very positive about teaching, and the experience of mentoring gave them a sense of renewal. They found the training component of the teacher-induction programs to be helpful but found scheduling a difficult aspect of the mentoring experience.

Tellez, K. T. 1992. Mentors by choice, not design: Help-seeking by beginning teachers. *Journal of Teacher Education* 43(3): 214–21.

This researcher studied teachers in an alternative-preparation program and found that almost all felt comfortable asking for help, but not always from their assigned mentor. Respondents were selective in asking for help, seeking friendly, caring, and not overly critical people. The researcher concludes that having a mentor seems to "encourage help-seeking, even if the mentor is not the one sought out." Some possible reasons for not asking a mentor teacher for help include: "embarrassment regarding asking for help"; "inaccessibility to mentors"; and "not overwhelmingly satisfied with mentors."

Trang, M. L., and F. A. Head. 1989a. Mentoring: The institutionalization of a natural process. *Eastern Education Journal* (Winter): 2–7.

Institutionalizing a process as complex and "squishy" as mentoring in a truly meaningful way is difficult at best. These authors discuss principles that can guide program developers as they implement mentoring programs in institutional settings.

Trang, M. L., and F. A. Head. 1989b. Educator views of professional commitment. *Texas Study of Secondary Education Research Journal* 42(2): 20–24.

Teacher educators often lament the fact that many teachers do not see themselves as teacher educators. This ethnographic study examines teachers' views of their professional commitment and how these presuppositions affect their mentoring practices.

Weeks, P. V. 1992. A mentor's point of view. *Intervention in School and Clinic* 27(5): 303–06.

An educational diagnostician who served as mentor to a first-year special education teacher describes her experiences, focusing on her overwhelming sense of responsibility, mentorship training, and critical incidents. The mentor's role in providing guidance without being evaluative is stressed, and development of a collegial mentor/protégé relationship is noted.

Wildman, T. M., S. G. Magliaro, R. A. Niles, and J. A. Niles. 1992. Teacher mentoring: An analysis of roles, activities, and conditions. *Journal of Teacher Education* 43(3): 205–13.

Mentors' notes and comments were analyzed to determine their perceptions of roles, activities, and conditions influencing their work with beginning teachers. Mentors had many helping strategies that developed and shaped complex roles. A conceptual framework of eight categories of mentoring activities addressing five domains of beginning teachers' concerns is proposed.

Wilkinson, G. A. 1994. Support for individualizing teacher induction. *Action in Teacher Education* 16(2): 52–61.

This study examines the types and amounts of assistance desired by beginning teachers. Surveys of beginning secondary teachers suggest that mentors must consider beginning teachers' needs and desires when determining the types and amounts of assistance provided. The study supports the need to vary the quantity and type of assistance provided for novices.

Williams, J. 1999. Guide, philosopher, friend (First appointments: Training for mentors of trainees and newly qualified teachers). *Times Educational Supplement* (London), 8 January, D30(2).

The training for both mentors to trainees and newly qualified teachers in British schools is inconsistent. An increasingly urgent need for good trainee mentors and induction mentors for newly qualified teachers exists. Therefore, more funding must be made available for high-quality training for mentors. It is particularly important that mentors are able to establish good working relationships with the universities responsible for training teachers.

Wise, A. E. 1997. New teachers say they are well prepared: Study in Kentucky reveals progress; NCATE a factor. *Quality Teaching* 6: 1–2.

Of more than 1,000 teachers prepared at NCATE institutions, 90 percent indicated that they were very well prepared, well prepared, or moderately well prepared to: establish a positive learning environment; communicate high expectations; design developmentally appropriate instruction; use different teaching strategies for different instructional purposes; and communicate the core concepts of their disciplines. About 70 percent of the principals said that these teachers had received more complete preparation than they themselves had.

JOURNAL THEME ISSUES ON MENTORING (1985–99)

Journal of Teacher Education, Volume 37, Number 1 (January–February 1985)
Educational Leadership, Volume 43, Number 3 (November 1985)
Kappa Delta Pi Record, Volume 22, Number 4 (Summer 1986)
Theory into Practice, Volume 25, Number 3 (Summer 1986)
Action in Teacher Education, Volume 8, Number 4 (Winter 1987)
Journal of Staff Development, Volume 11, Number 4 (Fall 1990)
Educational Horizons, Volume 73, Number 3 (Spring 1995)
Educational Leadership, Volume 56, Number 8 (May 1999)

MONOGRAPHS PRODUCED BY PROFESSIONAL ORGANIZATIONS (1985–99)

Brooks, D. M., ed. 1987. *Teacher induction: A new beginning:* Reston, Va.: Association of Teacher Educators.

The combined effect of these chapters is a needs-through-systems-to-recommendations synthesis of teacher induction. Chapters include:
Preface (Douglas M. Brooks)
Teacher Induction (Leslie Huling-Austin)
Local Induction Programs (Ralph Kester and Mary Marochie)
State-Wide Teacher Induction Programs (Parmalee Hawk and Shirley Robards)
The Role of Institutions of Higher Education in Professional Teacher Induction (John M. Johnston and Richard Kay)
Teacher Induction: Rationale and Issues (Sandra J. Odell)

Huling-Austin, L., S. J. Odell, P. Ishler, R. S. Kay, and R. A. Edelfelt, eds. 1989. *Assisting the beginning teacher.* Reston, Va: Association of Teacher Educators.

The purpose of this book is to help practitioners and policy makers understand how important it is to assist beginning teachers, and what it involves in terms of policy, procedures, pitfalls, personnel, price in time and money, and prospects. Chapters include:
Beginning Teacher Assistance Programs: An Overview (Leslie Huling-Austin)

Developing Support Programs for Beginning Teachers (Sandra J. Odell)

Research on Beginning Teacher Assistance Programs (Leslie Huling-Austin)

Impact of Beginning Teacher Assistance Programs (Peggy Ishler and Roy A. Edelfelt)

Evaluation of Beginning Teacher Assistance Programs (Richard S. Kay)

Starting a Beginning Teacher Assistance Program (Roy A. Edelfelt and Peggy Ishler)

Bey, T. M., and C. T. Holmes. 1990. Mentoring: Developing successful new teachers. Reston, Va.: Association of Teacher Educators.

This first mentoring monograph by the ATE Commission on the Role and Preparation of Mentor Teachers included the following chapters:
Support for New Teachers (Sandra J. Odell)
A Definition for Developing Self-Reliance (Richard S. Kay)
Mentoring Is Squishy Business (Leslie Huling-Austin)
A New Knowledge Base for Old Practice (Theresa M. Bey)
A Recapitulation (C. Thomas Holmes)

Bey, T. M., and C. T. Holmes. 1992. *Mentoring: Contemporary principles and issues.* Reston, Va.: Association of Teacher Educators.

This monograph was the second product of the ATE Commission on the Role and Preparation of Mentor Teachers. Chapters discuss the following topics:
Introduction: Why Mentoring Principles (Leslie Huling-Austin)
The Reality of Mentoring: Complexity in Its Process and Function (Fay A. Head, Alan J. Reiman, and Lois Thies-Sprinthall)
Psychological Support for Mentors and Beginning Teachers: A Critical Dimension (Yvonne Gold)
Mentoring: A Teacher Development Activity That Avoids Formal Evaluation of the Protégé (Judith C. Neal)
Mentor-Management: Emphasizing the HUMAN in Managing Human Resources (Richard S. Kay)
Guidelines for Selecting Mentors (Billie J. Enz)
Collaboration and Mentoring (Alan J. Reiman, Fay A. Head, and Lois Thies-Sprinthall)
Evaluating Mentoring Programs (Sandra J. Odell)
Designing Training and Selecting Incentives for Mentor Programs (Delores M. Wolfe)
Mentoring in Teacher Education: Diversifying Support for Teachers (Theresa M. Bey)

ERIC Documents Related to the Mentoring Framework (1985–99)

Achinstein, B., and T. Meyer. 1997. The uneasy marriage between friendship and critique: Dilemmas of fostering critical friendship in a novice teacher learning community. Paper presented at the Annual Meeting of the American Educational Research Association, Chicago, 24–28 March. ERIC ED 412 188.

Anctil, M. 1991. Mentor accountability: Acting in accordance with established standards. Paper presented at the Annual Meeting of the American Educational Research Association, Chicago, 3–7 April. ERIC ED 334 162.

Bennett, N., E. Dunne, and G. Harvard. 1995. The impact of training and role differentiation on the nature and quality of mentoring processes. Paper presented at the Annual Meeting of the American Educational Research Association, San Francisco, 18–22 April. ERIC ED 383 667.

Bower, A. M. 1990. Formalized mentoring relationships: Do they work? Paper presented at the Academy for Leadership in Teacher Education of the Association of Teacher Educators. Anaheim, Calif., 31 May–3 June. ERIC ED 326 487.

Bracht, G., and M. Peters. 1989. Minnesota's teacher mentorship program. Formative evaluation report. St. Paul: Minnesota State Department of Education. ERIC ED 349 273.

Brock, B. L., and M. L. Grady. 1996. Beginning teacher induction programs. Paper presented at the Annual Meeting of the National Council of Professors in Educational Administration, Corpus Christi, Tex., 6–10 August. ERIC ED 399 631.

Cantor, J. 1997. The development of beginning teachers as social justice educators in the context of a school-university partnership. Paper presented at the Annual Meeting of the American Educational Research Association, Chicago, 24–28 March. ERIC ED 408 270.

Ganser, T. 1994. How mentors rank mentor roles, benefits of mentoring and obstacles to mentoring. Paper presented at the Annual Meeting of the Association of Teacher Educators, Atlanta, 12–16 February. ERIC ED 367 631.

Ganser, T. 1997. The contribution of service as a cooperating teacher and mentor teacher to the professional development of teachers. Paper presented at the Annual Meeting of the American Educational Research Association, Chicago, 24–28 March. ERIC ED 408 279.

Ginns, I. S., and J. J. Watters. 1996. Experiences of novice teachers: Changes in self-efficacy and their beliefs about teaching. Paper presented at the Annual Meeting of the American Educational Research Association, New York, 8–12 April. ERIC ED 400 243.

Harper, S. L. 1988. An annotated bibliography of current literature on the mentoring of teachers: Collegial mentoring promotes dual professional growth. South Bend: Indiana University at South Bend. ERIC ED 311 029.

Klug, B. J., and S. A. Salzman. 1990. Formal induction vs. informal mentoring: Comparative effects and outcomes. Paper presented at the Annual Meeting of the American Educational Research Association, Boston, 16–20 April. ERIC ED 323 628.

Looney, J. 1997. Mentoring the beginning teacher: A study of influencing variables. Paper presented at the Annual Meeting of the Eastern Education Research Association, Hilton Head, S.C., February. ERIC ED 411 238.

Manthei, J. 1992. The mentor teacher as leader: The motives, characteristics and needs of seventy-three experienced teachers who seek a new leadership role. Paper presented at the Annual Meeting of the American Educational Research Association, San Francisco, 20–24 April. ERIC ED 346 042.

Meister, G. R. 1990. Help for new teachers: Developmental practices that work. Philadelphia: Research for Better Schools. ERIC ED 360 749.

O'Connor, E. A., and M. C. Fish. 1997. Differences between the classrooms of expert and novice teachers on the dimensions of the 'Classroom Systems Observation Scale.' Paper presented at the Annual Meeting of the New England Educational Research Organization, Portsmouth, N.H., 30 April–2 May. ERIC ED 409 307.

Parker, M. B. 1990. Adolescent dancing and the mentoring of beginning teachers. East Lansing: Michigan State University, National Center for Research on Teacher Learning. ERIC ED 327 515.

Reiman, A. J., and R. A. Edelfelt. 1990. School-based mentoring programs. Untangling the tensions between theory and practice. Research Report 90-7. Raleigh: North Carolina State University. ERIC ED 329 520.

Riggs, I., R. Sadlin, L. Scott, L. Childress, and D. E. Mitchell. 1997. The new teacher portfolio: A bridge to professional development. Paper presented at the Annual Meeting of the American Educational Research Association, Chicago, 24–28 March. ERIC ED 412 235.

Rothenberg, J. J., P. McDermott, and K. Gormley. 1997. Preparing white teachers for urban schools: A compendium of research. Paper presented at the Annual Meeting of the American Educational Research Association, Chicago, 24–28 March. ERIC ED 407 455.

Shepston, T. J. K., and R. A. Jensen. 1997. Dodging bullets and BMWs: Two tales of teacher induction. Paper presented at the Annual Meeting of the American Educational Research Association, Chicago, 24–28 March. ERIC ED 407 364.

Spuhler, L., and A. Zetler. 1995. Montana beginning teacher support program. Final report. Helena: Montana State Board of Education. ERIC ED 390 804.

Tauer, S. M. 1996. The mentor-protégé relationship and its effects on the experienced teacher. Paper presented at the Annual Meeting of the American Educational Research Association, New York, 8–12 April. ERIC ED 397 004.

Thompson, J. P. 1991. Integrating the mentorship factor into the clinical supervision model. Paper presented at the Annual Meeting of the Southwest Educational Research Association, Austin, Tex., 23–25 January. ERIC ED 411 235.

Tusin, L. F. 1995. Success in the first year of teaching: Effects of a clinical experience program. Paper presented at the Annual Meeting of the Association of Teacher Educators, Detroit, 21 February. ERIC ED 399 216.

Yosha, P. 1991. The benefits of an induction program: What do mentors and novices say? Paper presented at the Annual Meeting of the American Educational Research Association, Chicago, 3–7 April. ERIC ED 332 994.

DISSERTATIONS RELATED TO THE MENTORING FRAMEWORK (1985–99)

Andes, A. L. 1995. Mentoring: A component of new teacher induction. Ed.D. diss., Northern Arizona University.

Brumm, C. K. 1995. Correlations between induction program variables and the perceived effectiveness and satisfaction of beginning teachers. Ed.D. diss., University of LaVerne.

Burch, C. R. 1993. The early years of teaching: A study of the conditions affecting beginning teacher retention. Ed.D. diss., University of LaVerne.

Choo, V.-M. 1996. Teachers in transition: First-year teachers' perceptions of the contributions of collegiality to their growth. Ph.D. diss., Michigan State University.

Dagenais, R. J. 1990. A study of selected ability physical and psychological variables and the achievement of a successful mentoring experience. Ed.D. diss., Northern Illinois University.

Felton-Montgomery, P. A. 1994. 'Right from the start': A study of New Jersey's induction programs for beginning teachers. Ed.D. diss., Teachers College, Columbia University.

Guerra, M. M. 1994. The Texas induction year program as viewed by mentor and protégé participants in select districts in the Rio Grande Valley. Ed.D. diss., University of Houston.

Hartley, M. J. 1996. Mapping the organizational socialization and concerns of beginning teachers. Ed.D. diss., University of Northern Colorado.

Head, F. A. S. 1994. Modifying moral dilemmas for mentors and supervising teachers: An initial validation study of a cognitive developmental assessment model. Ed.D. diss., North Carolina State University.

Heathcoat, L. H. 1997. Teachers' early years: Context, concerns, and job satisfaction. Ed.D. diss., North Carolina State University.

Horton, N. C. 1997. Challenges to first year secondary science teachers. Ed.D. diss., University of Alabama.

Larsen, S. J. 1997. The effectiveness of teacher induction programs in improving the communication, management and socializational skills of new teachers. Ph.D. diss., Marquette University.

Lasinski, K. Z. 1992. A study of the differences in the self-reported induction needs of novice and system-new experienced elementary teachers and the teacher-preferred induction strategies to meet the reported needs. Ph.D. diss., American University.

Maddex, J. S. 1993. Survey of ten mentoring programs in Virginia. Ed.D. diss., Virginia Polytechnic Institute and State University.

Martin, M. J. 1997. The elementary principal and teacher induction: An explanatory case study using Fullan's strategies of change. Ed.D. diss., Oklahoma State University.

Melgarejo, E. T. 1992. An analysis of perceived significant learning experiences of beginning teachers. Ph.D. diss., the University of Maryland.

Pappalardo, R. 1996. The formal and informal socialization process of first-year teachers. Ed.D. diss., Arizona State University.

Rozario, G. M. 1995. An analysis of the new teacher induction program in the Madera Unified School District. Ed.D. diss., University of San Francisco.

Sanford, M. D. 1993. The beginning teacher: The first year's experience. Ph.D. diss., Syracuse University.

Schmidt, W. K. 1992. A study of the interrelationships of beginning teachers' perceptions of mentor support, teacher satisfaction and teacher concerns within a formal induction program. Ed.D. diss., Southern Illinois University.

Selke, M. J. G. 1992. Teacher induction variables: Impact upon second year teacher retention. Ph.D. diss., Marquette University.

Stewart, L. Y. 1997. New teacher induction and support: A comparison of program requirements as perceived by beginning teachers and district personnel officers. Ed.D. diss., University of Southern California.

Wang, J. 1998. Learning to teach mathematics: Preservice teachers, their collaborating teachers and instructional contexts. Ph.D. diss., Michigan State University.

Wong-Park, M. G. 1997. The relationship between assessment procedures in teacher support programs and teachers' feelings of support. Ed.D. diss., University of LaVerne.

LITERATURE FROM OTHER ACADEMIC DISCIPLINES RELATED TO THE MENTORING FRAMEWORK

Boice, R. 1992. Lessons learned about mentoring. In *Developing new and junior faculty,* ed. M. D. Sorcinelli and A. E. Austin, 51–61. San Francisco: Jossey-Bass.

Daloz, L. A. 1987. *Effective teaching and mentoring: Realizing the transformational power of adult learning experiences.* San Francisco: Jossey-Bass.

Gray, W. A., and M. M. Gray. 1986. *Mentoring: Aid to excellence in career development, business, and the professions.* Burnaby, B.C.: International Association for Mentoring.

Haring-Hidore, M. 1987. Mentoring as a career enhancement strategy for women. *Journal of Counseling & Development* 66(6): 147–48.

Klauss, R. 1981. Formalized mentor relationships for management and executive development programs in the federal government. *Public Administration Review* 41(4): 489–96.

Kram, K. E. 1983. Phases of the mentor relationship. *Academy of Management Journal* 26(4): 608–25.

Kram, K. E., and L. A. Isabella. 1985. Mentoring alternatives: The role of peer relationships in career development. *Academy of Management Journal* 28(1): 110–32.

Lambert, D., and L. Lambert. 1985. Mentor teachers as change facilitators.

Thrust 14(6): 28–32.

Levinson, D. J., C. N. Darrow, E. B. Klein, M. H. Levinson, B. McKee. 1978. *The seasons of a man's life.* New York: Knopf.

Merriam, S. 1983. Mentors and protégés: A critical review of the literature. *Adult Education Quarterly* 33(3): 161–73.

Phillips-Jones, L. L. 1983. Establishing formalized mentoring programs. *Training and Development Journal* 37(2): 38–42.

Zey, M. 1984. *The mentor connection.* Homewood, Ill.: Dow Jones-Irwin.

NOTES

About the Authors

Carol A. Bartell has teaching and administrative experience at the elementary, secondary, and university levels. Her research and writing is focused primarily on professional mentoring and induction. She is the Dean of the School of Education at California Lutheran University, which produces approximately 250 teachers, administrators, counselors, and curriculum specialists each year. Dr. Bartell currently serves as the President of the California Council on the Education of Teachers, the oldest and largest professional association of teacher educators in the state. Prior to becoming Dean, Dr. Bartell worked in a state policy role for the California Commission on Teacher Credentialing, with primary responsibility for California's Beginning Teacher Support and Assessment program. She led the development of program standards and the California Standards for the Teaching Profession. Dr. Bartell is currently managing the development and evaluation of a peer-review system for program improvement.

Barbara D. Day is Professor and Chair of Curriculum and Instruction at the University of North Carolina, Chapel Hill. Among other books, she has authored *Early Childhood Education: Developmental/Experiential Teaching and Learning,* 4th ed., and *Good Schools for Young Children,* 5th ed. She also co-authored *Early Childhood Education: Curriculum Organization and Classroom Management.* As chair of the International Research Committee of the Delta Kappa Gamma Society International, she authored *Education for the 21st Century—Key Issues: Leadership, Literacy, Legislation and Learning.* She served as an Advisor on ASCD's 1991 video staff-development program, a videotape program and Facilitator's

Manual that won the CINE Golden Eagle Award. Along with leadership roles in ASCD, Dr. Day is currently serving as President of Kappa Delta Pi, International Honor Society in Education. In 1999, she served as editor for the KDP Biennial Theme Book, *Teaching and Learning in the New Millennium*.

Gary P. DeBolt is Assistant Superintendent for Curriculum and Instruction for the Fairport Central School District in Fairport, New York. Previously, Dr. DeBolt served as the Director of the Ella Cline Shear School of Education at the State University of New York at Geneseo. He has taught at the university level for ten years and is a 14-year veteran of middle and high school social studies teaching. Dr. DeBolt's research interests center on mentoring for new teachers. He is the editor of two books, *Teacher Induction and Mentoring: School-Based Collaborative Programs* (1992) and *United Nations Curriculum Guide* (1995).

Janet Dynak is the Dean of the School of Education at Westminster College in Salt Lake City. She has been a faculty member at Western Michigan University, special education teacher, general education teacher, curriculum director, and reading consultant in Michigan and in Germany with the Department of Defense Overseas Schools. Dr. Dynak co-directed a Preparation of Personnel for Careers in Special Education Federal Grant that helped fund the Transdisciplinary Collaboration Preparation Program at Western Michigan University. She also has been actively involved in several Michigan Campus Compact Grants to support a variety of mentoring programs in local school districts throughout Michigan. Dr. Dynak currently serves on the Executive Board of the Northern Rocky Mountain Educational Research Association. Her professional interests include curriculum reform in teacher education as it relates to collaborative initiatives with K–12 schools. Her many publications reflect an interest in action research as it relates to self-study and mentoring of preservice teachers.

Sharon Feiman-Nemser is a Professor of Teacher Education at Michigan State University, where she teaches undergraduate and graduate courses, works in a professional-development school, and pursues research and scholarly interests in teacher learning and teacher education. Dr. Feiman-Nemser is one of the faculty directors of MSU's five-year, field-based teacher education program. She focuses her work on developing the yearlong internship. She previously carried out studies about learning to teach and mentoring practices at the National Center for Research on Teacher Education. She is currently directing a national study of exemplary induction programs under the auspices of the National Partnership for Excellence and Accountability and writing a book on mentored learning to teach. Dr. Feiman-Nemser has written extensively on teacher education, learning to teach, mentoring, and induction. Dr. Feiman-Nemser is a past recipient of the AACTE Margaret Lindsey Award for outstanding research and a Distinguished Faculty Award at Michigan State.

Fay A. Head is an adjunct professor at Webster University in Myrtle Beach, South Carolina. Her long-standing interest in mentoring is reflected by experience and education in mentoring, outreach, professional development, and integration of educational ideas across disciplines and the whole spectrum of human development. She has served on the Association of Teacher Educators' National Commission on the Role and Preparation of Mentor Teachers and the Commission on Character Education. Dr. Head has published monograph chapters and articles on mentoring, teacher induction, and moral development. In addition, she has established and directed exemplary programs to enhance teaching excellence; assess and improve second-language skills for international teaching assistants; prepare doctoral students and new professors for the professorate; and coordinate professional-development systems.

Leslie Huling is Associate Dean of Education at Southwest Texas State University. Prior to joining the Department of Curriculum and Instruction at SWT in 1986, she was a program director at the Research and Development Center for Teacher Education at the University of Texas at Austin. As director, she served as the principal investigator of the Model Teacher Induction Project Study and the Teacher Induction in Diverse Contexts Study, a collaborative research study involving 26 national sites. She has served on the Association of Teacher Educator's Commissions on the Teacher Induction Process, the Role and Preparation of Mentor Teachers, and co-chairs the Commission of Professional Support and Development for Novice

Teachers. She has provided teacher induction preparation to educators from more than 30 states and Canada. Dr. Huling is co-author of three books on teacher induction and author of numerous articles on mentoring in a wide variety of journals. Recently, she was the co-editor of the eight-volume *Restructuring Texas Teacher Education Series,* published in 1998.

Anne L. Nagel has served as a faculty member at Oregon State University, Michigan State University, and San Diego State University. In her current position at San Diego State, she serves as Faculty Team Leader for the Alliance for Excellence field-based teacher education program. This program won the top award in the Association of Teacher Educators Distinguished Program competition in 1986. Dr. Nagel has been active at the local, state, and national levels in the Association of Teacher Educators, the International Reading Association, and Kappa Delta Pi. She has been selected as Outstanding Professor in Teacher Education at the university on four different occasions. Dr. Nagel served for five years as Co-Director of the San Diego Beginning Teacher Support and Assessment Program and is currently involved in establishing new BTSA programs in San Diego County.

Sandra J. Odell is currently a Professor of Education at the University of Nevada, Las Vegas, and has been Professor and Director of Undergraduate Studies at Western Michigan University and a faculty member at the University of New Mexico. Dr. Odell has authored *Mentor Teacher Programs,* chapters in several monographs and books, as well as many journal articles on the topics of teacher induction and mentoring. The first three Association of Teacher Educator Yearbooks were co-edited by Dr. Odell. She has served on the ATE National Commissions on Teacher Induction and the Role and Preparation of Mentor Teachers. Dr. Odell currently co-chairs the Commission on Professional Support and Development for Novice Teachers. She is the recipient of the 1999 ATE and Wadsworth Publishing Co. Distinguished Teacher Educator award and is Past President of the Nevada Association of Teacher Educators. Dr. Odell maintains career-long research interests in teacher development, teacher induction, and mentoring in the context of collaborative university/ school district programs.

Alan J. Reiman is currently an Associate Professor in the Department of Curriculum and Instruction at North Carolina State University. He was an elementary teacher in rural and urban schools for several years before working as a clinical associate professor jointly with Wake County Public Schools and North Carolina State University. During that time, he supported a yearlong professional-development program for aspiring mentors based on cognitive-developmental theory. He organized a large consortium across seven school districts that sought better ways to support beginning teachers and counselors. Dr. Reiman has published numerous journal articles and book chapters related to adult development, teacher professional development, mentoring, and teacher reflection. His research interests include investigations of how professional roles and reflection promote educator intellectual, interpersonal, and ethical development. He is the co-author of *Mentoring and Supervision for Teacher Development.*

Virginia Resta is an Associate Professor in the Department of Curriculum and Instruction at Southwest Texas State University, San Marcos. Her areas of expertise include teacher education in reading, language arts, and technology. Dr. Resta has been a teacher, clinical supervisor, and reading coordinator for a large urban school system. She has extensive experience in field-based preservice and graduate-level teacher education programs. She is currently coordinating a field-based professional-development exchange program for first-year and experienced teachers. Dr. Resta has authored several articles in the areas of mentoring and school/university collaboration.

Sharon A. Schwille is a senior academic specialist in the Department of Teacher Education in the College of Education at Michigan State University. She coordinates the Teacher Preparation Program and works with interns and collaborating teachers in schools. In past years, she coordinated both the standard and alternative teacher-preparation programs at Michigan State. Her research interests focus on teacher learning and guided practice, especially mentoring of preservice and induction year teachers. Recently, she worked on a comparative, cross-cultural study, Learning from Mentors, sponsored by the National Center for Research on Teacher Learning. Currently, she is involved in a national study of exemplary induction programs as part of the National Partnership for Excellence and Accountability in Teaching.

Barry W. Sweeny is an independent educational consultant with Best Practice Resources in Wheaton, Illinois. He has been a consultant, facilitator, and author, working with dozens of school districts, professional associations, colleges, regional agencies, and nonprofit organizations and as a presenter and keynote speaker at conferences throughout the United States. He is probably best known for his mentor preparation materials, his mentoring Web site at *www.teachermentors.com,* and his role in founding the Association of Supervision and Curriculum Development Mentoring Leadership and Resource Network *(www.mentors.net).* He also works in the areas of school improvement, peer coaching, staff development, and performance-based teaching, learning, and assessment. Previously, he was a classroom teacher, district staff developer, mentor-program coordinator, and Manager of School and Program Development at two different Regional Offices of Education in Illinois. He is also Past President of the Illinois Staff Development Council.

Michael P. Wolfe is Executive Director of Kappa Delta Pi, International Honor Society in Education, serving 60,000 members. He has authored more than 60 journal articles and book chapters on teacher effectiveness, school climate, and effective schools. He has co-authored *Critical Incidents in School Administration* and co-edited *Life Cycle of the Career Teacher.* Dr. Wolfe has been a public school teacher and program coordinator and has served as a professor of teacher education and administrator at Central Michigan University, Texas Christian University, and SUNY Plattsburgh. Dr. Wolfe has recently been elected President of the Association of College Honor Societies, representing 65 different honor societies and 4.5 million members. Dr. Wolfe has been an active contributor to numerous school districts throughout the United States as a consultant on effective schools, school improvement, creating positive school climate, enhancing self-concept, and teacher-induction practices.